ONE IN SEVEN?

One man's fight

Nick 'JJ' Allan

This book is dedicated to the children and partners of alcoholics. It recognises the pain and suffering which the drink dependent cause to themselves and, ultimately to those around them. If you survive by recognising your dilemma and successfully dealing with it – be proud. If you struggle, be comforted in the knowledge that you're not alone.

This book is also dedicated to male victims of domestic abuse, violence and control. You may be met by institutional disbelief, distrust and contempt. If you're a father, you may even have your children used against you, or worse, lose them. My message is don't lose heart. Your unspoken suffering isn't unique. In large part, that is why this book has been written. For a woman, there is support and written material. For a man, there is little help available and little willing to be offered. I want to address this and, if you take anything from it, learn to put pride aside, be honest with yourself, be true to yourself and never be afraid to share. You are the rock on which the rest of your life is built.

TURNING POINT

It could have been a horror movie. I knew it was happening, but I couldn't feel it... at least not right there in the moment. The amount of blood on my face told me for sure that I was hurt, but the kicks to my head, sides, and hips seemed strangely painless. I tried to curl into a ball to protect myself, but my attacker grabbed my hair from behind and ripped it out by the roots. That I did feel! I managed break free as blood trickled down my face and onto the living room carpet. Then, stumbling into the kitchen, I was confronted by a sight which made the last few moments seem tame.

The young boy stood, trembling and staring at us with wide dark, eyes. His pale face expressed the shock at what he was seeing. His slender young fingers grasped the hilt of a carving knife, which he pressed point first into the skin of his throat.

"STOP .... STOP IT! .... LEAVE MY DAD ALONE!".

A new determination took over. I had to tell him that I was OK... dad was OK ...... everything would be OK. But he'd seen it all before ... he'd heard it all before .... things no 8-year-old child should ever have to witness. I knew that this was it and it could go on no longer. My priority was him and to hell with the consequences, now. The

time for cowardly, passive tolerance was over. I was ashamed, deeply ashamed, for what I'd allowed to become familiar.

"STOP IT NOW ... I'LL KILL MYSELF!"

The pain was kicking in now, my heart was pounding and I was breathless and trembling. In that instant, though, I knew what to do. Darting past my attacker, I ran for the second door in the living room, knowing that they would follow my distraction. Circling back into the kitchen along the passage, I grabbed Jack and gathered him into my arms, forcing the knife from his small fingers which gripped it with unbelievable strength. I limped into the hallway and out of the front door, down the steps and into the garden. The escape attempt was frantic and agonising. I was in my late forties, overweight and unfit. My legs felt like lead and it seemed that I was hardly moving – like one of those nightmares where you're running from an unknown terror but making no progress. This terror, though, wasn't unknown, it was dreadfully well known to me.

There was no time to look for my keys and no time to waste in getting into my small van and starting it. We had to get out of there NOW. It was late afternoon but too early for any of the neighbours to be around. Most worked and weren't yet home. All we could do on that cold March Friday – was run!

THE JOURNEY BEGINS

How the hell did I get here? To this point in my life ... to these incredible events.

My early life couldn't have been more different. Born into an extended, warm and loving family, I lived with mam and dad at my maternal grandparents' house on the family market garden which was in a small pit village in northwest Durham. I was also surrounded by a host of loving aunts and uncles, too.

At the age of three, my parents bought a new house, a few miles to the north. I didn't take to the move well, being wrenched from that ancient farmhouse despite its lack of creature comforts such as a bath and an inside loo. The new home was a great financial burden to mam and dad, being all of £2,500! However, it was a large modern semi and came with 'mod cons'. As was the way, mam was the homemaker and converted the shell into a true home. Dad was a miner but had been forced to the surface the year of my birth, thanks to an accident with a conveyor, leaving him with a serious arm injury, which was 'repaired' using a metal wrist 'bone'. In his new daylight environment, he became head gardener for the colliery. He supplemented our income by continuing to work on the family market garden at weekends, and also for a nearby similar business when they need extra help. Because of this, then, dad was an unfamiliar figure within the family home. Both my parents were avid gardeners though. The new house was at the edge of an Edwardian pit spoil heap and dad negotiated with the National Coal Board, handing over the grand sum of £80 to buy ¼ acre of the land. Jump forward 40 years and you'd find a magical and breathtaking testimony to their dedication and expertise. It was a stunning landscaped explosion of colour and wonder which was even featured in the press and on local TV. In all ways, they worked as a formidable team, dad being the 'civil engineer' and mam, the horticultural artist.

Three years after the move, in the middle of one of the most brutal winters on record, my sister arrived in February. We hadn't yet the luxury of a phone, so at the age of six, I walked with dad through the deepest snow drifts I have ever seen, before or since, to fetch the midwife. Despite all, the baby arrived safely during a home birth. She was healthy – something that would be cruelly smashed apart 25 years later, with a diagnosis of multiple sclerosis.

In the meanwhile, however, the scene was set for a traditional and conventional childhood. We were at the centre of our parents' loving universe. Money was tight, of course. To this day, I recall mam scratching behind the fireplace to recover a lost half-crown so we could buy bread and a few groceries. Mondays were wash days, Sundays were roast dinner and baking days, Saturdays were family days and everyday was a house cleaning day. What we lacked in 'things' was more than offset by love, care, safety and inspiration.

The house was on a small, new estate. Being all of a similar age, the parents produced children who could play together, innocently in the wide-open spaces around us. There were 2 local schools and I'd been enrolled in the Church of England Parochial school at the age of 5.

There were the usual ups and downs of family life, but I came to be racked with guilt 40 years on, when I wasn't able to provide the same happiness and security for my own son. As a father, I would fail.

I was very close to mam, who was ever-present and my carer, teacher, entertainer and nurturer. Then, of course, there were my grandmother and aunts. Altogether, it was a matriarchal family although both mam and dad were the source of my inherited moral backbone and ethic for hard work. They were my role models and my rocks.

I was a painfully shy child when it came to

members of the opposite sex. Strange, you may think, for the product of a matriarchy. Women and girls were to be honoured and respected, but also to be obeyed and I even believed them to be 'superior'. In my teens, I was attracted to many girls as my hormones cut loose and rampaged around. However, I worshipped from afar for fear of being rejected. There was an air of vulnerability which resulted in one of the most painful experiences of my life. At the age of 14, while on a school trip, I was methodically teased, embarrassed and belittled by a succession of girls on the coach. They toyed with me, ruthlessly, egged on by the cock-sure male class heartthrobs. Sadness, anger and resentment inevitably followed. This was one of the turning points in my life. I was fast becoming a loner and the experience, in no small part, helped lead me to the place in which I eventually found myself. There were high points too, of course. Such as the day I was elevated to Head Boy in preference to one of my male tormentors who was not only a heartthrob but a talented sportsman. This prompted a complaint by the boy's parents who failed to see why the position had been given to a chubby, reserved geek. Nevertheless, with the support of the headmaster, I excelled, achieving good O and A Level results and even developing a respectable amount of self-confidence.

I went on to study for a degree in Economics at the then Newcastle Polytechnic while I continued to live at home and my school friends were off to their own universities and colleges or work and to develop their other interests. I entered local politics and while this took up a lot of my time and I achieved high local office (even standing 3 times as a candidate), the yearning for female companionship didn't go away. By the time I was 21, panic had set in with a fear of being 'left on the shelf'.

A year later, I was invited on a blind date by one of my friends and his girlfriend. My date was her work colleague. I agonised for a while but eventually agreed. We had a relaxed and enjoyable evening at a pub in Newcastle before going off for a meal. I wasn't particularly physically attracted to her and was fairly certain this would be a one-off. However, we did 'hit it off' in a friendly way and continued to meet. Things developed and then, another year later, and much to my relief, I lost my virginity between purple nylon sheets in a guest house in Keswick. It has to be said that the build-up of static electricity probably added to the experience, although this was somewhat of a busman's holiday because, by this time, I actually worked for Brentford Nylons, the manufacturers of said notable sheets. I had warned her I was a workaholic.

Wendy and I married 3 years later and we stayed together for 12 years, moving house several times. We built homes together and eventually became soul mates, caring deeply for each other. We couldn't have children, allegedly because my sperm was 'lazy'. So what? I thought. Better to have a slow saunter up and have a good time when you get there, rather than rush around and risk dying before you arrive! In truth, however, I was relieved. I didn't want to be a father but, unfairly, didn't share this with her. She did want a family of our own and, following her seeing a doctor, I was swept up in a storm of consultations, tests and, eventually an experimental IVF programme called GIFT. Not wanting to upset things, I foolishly went along with all of this. At hospital, I was bundled into supply cupboards with small bottles, by condescending nurses. It was my job to 'wank' into them (not all on one occasion I hasten to add) and reappear all smiles and victorious with the receptacles (which were always far bigger than I could possibly do them justice). Instead, I came out rather sheepishly, red faced and with trembling legs. I was also mentally exhausted because this was all done using my imagination. I couldn't 'get off' on staring at bed pans and catheters so was obliged to draw upon my limited experience. I was then shooed away into the side room to await Wendy's arrival from theater. This was my first experience as a slightly superfluous sperm donor. My presence might have been necessary, but I wasn't really a part of the process. Animal husbandry is more thoughtful and civilized. Yet another traumatic life experience ......

From my point of view, this was the start of the death of our marriage. Not only did we want different things, but I realised that I was just no longer in love with Wendy, if I ever had been. I admired and respected her but perhaps, when we got married, I'd unwittingly started out on a road which would define my life to date. I'd been unfair to both of us. It had been another momentous turning point.

Over the following 3 years, we grew further apart. The strain on the relationship was extreme and neither of us was happy. At this point, something happened to change everything. I was about to press the nuclear button.

12 YEAR ITCH

By the age of 37, my career had progressed in leaps and bounds. I was Trading Controller for the textile arm of a multinational trading company. I was responsible for all buying and sales operations and one of 3 senior executives. My job took me all over the country. The hotel life suited me. I was a workaholic and didn't relish the prospect of being at home in a loveless relationship. We had it all – large new house, 2 cars, excellent salaries, bonus, smart suits, a holiday cottage and lots of 'things'. All I lacked was inner peace and contentment. Perhaps I'd sold my soul to the devil?

Despite the outward appearance of success, however, I was still shy and reserved with members of the opposite sex. I hid it well and no one who worked with me could have known how racked with self-doubt I was.

A few years earlier, I'd employed a young local girl as a clerk typist. I didn't take anything but a professional interest in her. However, now, she'd blossomed into a young woman in her twenties and my marriage was loveless and sexless.

Judith, later my second wife, started showing a personal interest in me beyond work. I couldn't accept that a young attractive girl could be remotely interested in me. However, she gradually wore down my guard, constantly making me coffee, spending time in my office, asking about my marriage and getting quite close to me.

I had a policy of having head office staff spend at least a couple of days a year in the field at one of our shops. This was to experience the customer facing side of our business. One of my fellow executives or I would take them to a shop, deposit them for a day and return later to collect them. On one such occasion, I took Judith and one of her colleagues to our branch in Edinburgh. After introducing them to the manager, I carried on to a series of meetings in Stirling and Dundee.

On collecting them for the return journey, Judith insisted on sitting directly behind the driver's seat. After about an hour, I became aware of her gently rubbing my back in the space between the seat and the door. The feel of her gentle touch was thrilling and the experience was beyond my wildest dreams. This was something I'd rarely, if ever, experienced. After a stop for a meal, I drove on, dropped off Judith's colleague and we continued to the coast. It was there, in my car, that our affair began. Judith brought me a new spark, sexual adventure and excitement. From that point on, it was a roller coaster of illicit trysts and sex. I was making up for lost time and putting my painful teens and twenties behind me.

Judith lived with her parents and, while she continued to see other men (we'd agreed to an 'open' relationship), they encouraged her to continue our affair (especially her mother). As it developed, I was less happy that Judith was seeing other men and her mother told her to give me an ultimatum to end my marriage and dedicate myself to her. I needed little encouragement but knew that it was going to be traumatic.

Along with the excitement came guilt and stress. My marriage was now dead and we were two people living under the same roof. Nevertheless, my conscience was making me ill because of my betrayal. Wendy didn't deserve this (although I later discovered she'd been doing the same for around the same length of time). It was time to come clean.

On the Wednesday before my 40th birthday, I went home early and packed some clothes. It was 5pm and I waited in silence for Wendy to get home. She usually arrived at between 530 and 6pm and my heart pounded in my chest as I waited. The long minutes extended to excruciating hours and still I sat, quiet, in the dark on that cold winter's day. At about 8, she finally arrived, surprised to see me as I rarely got back until after 10pm. I didn't ask where she'd been, although, looking back, I think I knew.

I told her that the marriage was over and that I was moving out. She was distraught – not because she loved me but because she NEEDED me. This was her own insecurity. She was a capable an independent woman. She was simply 'used' to me and obviously afraid about what the future would hold. She was so distraught that I couldn't bring myself to tell her about Judith. In my own insane logic, I thought this would destroy her even further. I could, at least, spare her that.

I left and drove the 35 miles to our holiday cottage in the Scottish borders. Over the next few weeks, I sank into a deep depression over what I'd done to Wendy. It was wrong and I'd hurt her deeply. However, my real sin was maybe to have married her in the first place. I'd used her to avoid being alone. THAT was dishonest and it was no basis for a relationship. My own insecurities had buggered up her life, to my shame. For that reason, I continued to pay all the household bills and, with the divorce settlement, I willingly walked away and left her with everything – the debris of our life together.

Despite my remorse, the relationship with Judith continued. I buried myself further into work. 2 years earlier, a competitor company had approached me, with very generous terms, to join them to develop their chain of shops. Because my present employer was now in the grasp of a fire and brimstone bigoted southerner, the decision had been made to relocate the non-manufacturing parts of the business to London. I was one of two executives the detestable dickhead from Dartford had asked to join him. Therefore, I grasped the new opportunity, setting up a local office staffed by some of my best people and, of course, Judith. The fact that I'd been able to secure a very generous redundancy package was the icing on the cake.

Before starting our torrid affair, I'd been aware of Judith's fondness for booze. Her wild exploits and binge drinking were the stuff of legends at work. I'd convinced myself that this was all youthful hi jinks and that she'd settle down. After all, she'd assured me that her parents hadn't allowed her to drink until she was 16, and only then, under their guidance. Oh, they guided her sure enough and this was all bollocks!

I saw her personality change radically when she was pissed. At a works Christmas function in Newcastle, she became a different person as the night wore on. This was the first time she hit me – twice as it happened, in the face. I'd been standing at the top of the stairs when she suddenly swung at me, sending me reeling down several steps before I caught my balance. I caught sight of her outside and, having forced herself to the front of a long queue, she proceeded to wrestle another girl and drag her out of a taxi so she and her friend could take it. She shouted at me to join them – an invitation which I declined. I was still married to Wendy and I wasn't going to push my luck any further.

After my breakup with Wendy and joining my new employer, our small team spent a lot of time living out of hotels in Lancashire, until the Gateshead office was set up. Our time was fully expensed and Judith in particular, really indulged in the mini bars, room service, and bars. I remember one such evening when, to her horror, the barman closed the bar at 10:30 pm, drawing down the security grille around it. But Judith, being highly motivated, managed to squeeze her slender hand through the grille, along with a glass, and reach the pump to pour herself another lager. She was so proud of herself and often told the story to anyone who would listen, for years to come. Throughout our remaining years together, she kept her love of the hotel life and always made an effort to stay away. By now, I'd grown my new company's branch numbers by a factor of 10 and sales by 9 times to

£17million. There were warning signs, of course – her frequent tirades at me in front of staff, her refusal to leave me alone to work in the office and even the odd punch to the side of the head. I grew to realise that she was lazy and often absent. I stupidly ignored these things and made excuses for her, but my reputation was collapsing. I had become a pathetic easy touch ... and the worst was yet to come.

ALL CHANGE

Almost 3 years passed and, despite the success of our small subsidiary, the parent company was in trouble. I suspected that something fundamental was going to happen, so it was time to build an escape route for myself and Judith

I wasn't yet divorced from Wendy, but we did have a separation agreement. At the same time, I'd joined my new employer, I'd found and bought a small 2 bedroomed detached bungalow close by. It was in a quiet, leafy and pleasant crescent off one of the steepest banks on Tyneside. The house was quite run down but, after 3 months hard slog, dad and I had transformed it into a nice modern home – if a bit 'blokey'. I wasn't one for frills and flounces. After all, it was going to be a female free zone ....
WRONG! Judith had stayed over the odd night after I'd moved in a few months before. Soon, an odd night had turned into most nights and then into every night. I wasn't ready for this but, once again, my weakness of will allowed it to happen. She became a permanent presence but brought nothing to the home, either financially or by effort. She believed that I'd take care of everything, and that was her guiding principle throughout our relationship, right up until the very end.

After moving in with me, I discovered that she walked and talked in her sleep, fuelled by drink. Early one morning, I was awakened by the sound of crashing and banging coming from the bathroom. My immediate thought was 'burglars' and, bravely, didn't even look over to Judith's side of the bed to make sure she was OK. Naked, I gingerly opened the bedroom door and crept into the hallway. A crack of light appeared from the bathroom. Suddenly, the door flung open! There followed an eerie sight of a typist chair slowly moving out, apparently under its own momentum. It stopped abruptly and shuddered and banged backwards and forwards. Could this be a haunting!? As the chair moved further out, two hands became visible on the back. Judith emerged, zombie like and also naked, her eyes wide open and glazed. She kept chanting "You can't blame me for this …. You can't blame me for this…" I slowly backed up, partly in puzzlement and partly in fright. My retreat was then brought to a sudden halt when my bare arse came into contact with a hot radiator. I screamed and she woke……..

Meanwhile, back at the ranch, our parent company had decided to draw our division into the main plant in Lancashire, to shore up the profitability. I didn't want to move to Nelson, so I decided to stay out of it. For the second time within 3 years, then, I walked away with another very generous redundance package.

My new life strategy was now to 'spread the risk' and not be dependent on an employer and certainly not a single employer. So, I decided to become a management consultant. I also had to think about what to do about Judith. She didn't seem to have any plans or reason to get a job so she could contribute. She was content to lie around the house, often with her parents in tow. I didn't find either palatable (either option, I mean). Because she was a competent copy typist, I spent a few thousand on computers and equipment to set her up in her own secretarial business. I also provided her with a car so she could travel around her clients. One of the 2 bedrooms was converted into a lovely office for her. A fair amount of money was spent on advertising and there was no shortage of business. All we lacked now was a worker!

True to form, work was the very last thing on Judith's mind. She could have made a good living and there were several lucrative and steady contracts initially. However, she simply couldn't motivate herself to put in the effort. Then was the final nail in the coffin – her parents. Dick and Janet started to visit every day, every week for 8 – 10 hours a day. Because I was out and about trying to earn a living, I didn't fully appreciate what was going on and that these two were to become 'poltergeists' in my life. Suffice it to say that whatever the season, the three of them sat around the gas fire, curtains drawn, lights on, watching TV, eating, and of course, drinking. Judith's business quickly withered and died.

In the meanwhile, its fair for you to ask – what was I doing?

Back in the 80s, dad had built a very successful little furniture restoration company. Having developed diabetes, he'd sold the business before he reached 60 but was still receiving an impressive number of calls and enquiries from his clients. I then had the notion to revive his business. I'd take care of all the administrative stuff, which he found so tiresome. I used a fair amount of my reserves to set up a larger company, backed by professional marketing, management and the best equipment. In addition, I 'head hunted' dad's old assistant. And so, in that same momentous year, Northern French Polishers was born!

In the early years, I knew that NFP wouldn't be able to sustain all of us. But, using my savings and income from the consultancy, I worked hard to develop it, drawing no income for 2 years. However, by year 3, dad's start up little enterprise had developed into the largest furniture restoration house in the northeast! I gave up the consultancy and concentrated on it full time, working over 60 hours a week. I even retrained myself and became a pretty good cabinet maker and furniture repairer. The polishing, though, I left to them 'that knew'.

One day, just before leaving for work, I found Judith crying in the bedroom. This was rare and I knew something was very wrong. The mail had just arrived and she showed me a credit card bill for £1000 which had a final demand attached to it. She couldn't pay it, not having an income now. In sympathy, but stupidly in hindsight, I paid it off for her. I didn't like seeing her distressed, but this was to be the first of many 'bailouts'. Yet again, I'd failed to heed the warnings.

Over the next 2 years, Northern tripled in size. I recruited extra staff and was playing an active part in production, as well as managing the business, collecting, delivering, estimating, selling and all the other things a busy owner does! I was the lowest paid and least skilled, but it was all mine! The future looked good!

Office work, unusually, became a burden to me now. I needed help and hit upon the naive idea that I could save Judith from herself (and her parents) and help the business in one fell swoop. She had a strong background in admin and payroll. By 'employing' her it also had the added benefit of me being able to 'keep an eye on her'. And so, it started quite successfully at first, although I'd forgotten about her lousy sense of direction and geography. She had me zig zagging across the north of England, following the most insane journey plans. I honestly thought she was simply sticking pins in the map at random. Nevertheless, I was able to hand over a great deal of the admin, tax, national insurance and bankings.

Still the business grew and I was forever chasing the next opportunity. As the demands grew, Judith suggested her father might be able to help around the workshop. Another fatal error. She paid him cash in hand without considering the implications. He was already on the top rate of incapacity benefit and had a mobility car, having persuaded the DWP that he had an incurable bad back before 'medically retiring' some 12 years before, at the age of 50. Between the pair of them, they were earning more than 3 times my 'wage'. Worse, though, was the harm they inflicted on the business and the rest of the team.

I became increasingly irritated to find Judith

and her father absent much of the time. While I was on the road by around 7:30 or 8:00 am, other team members told me that the pair of them usually arrived at work around 10:30 am and left 2 hours later. They continued to draw the same money, of course because Judith controlled the payroll. This had to stop.

One evening, I'd retuned to the office and again found calls unanswered and paperwork neglected. I drove home and found Dick alone, in front of the TV as usual, gas fire blazing. I asked where Judith was, to be told that she'd gone shopping with Janet. I went back to work to finish the stuff she hadn't. On returning home, there they were. Two gaggling and pissed witches. This was their lifestyle and this was where my hard-earned funds were going.

Rows were aplenty. But there were always excuses. I was being treated like a joke, laughed at, and ridiculed. As a result of my work schedule and the long hours I spent on the road, my home was being turned into a biblical hell hole like Gomorrah, in my absence. Soon, though, they'd have another weapon they would use against me – and this time it was truly devastating!

JACK

Two years had gone by since "we" had moved into the new house.

Despite being on the pill, Judith suddenly announced that she was pregnant. Whilst I wasn't 'ready' because of my mounting concerns, I was 41 and getting on. Besides, the material circumstances were all in place – a house and a business and reasonable income. I was accountable to no one and started looking forward to being a father.

Judith was due to be induced on 18th June. I'd gone to work early to set up the schedules for the day before travelling up to the maternity unit, where I was 'welcomed' by her mother and told to wait until I was called by the midwife. She then disappeared. In fact, she'd engineered the situation to keep me far enough away to be ignorant of the fact that the delivery was about to start. Having told the delivery team that I hadn't turned up, she then installed herself in the delivery suite herself, instead of me. But then things went wrong.

The first inkling I had that all wasn't right was when I saw Judith, on a surgical trolley, being rushed past the door. The baby was stuck and she needed an emergency caesarian. She was losing a great deal of blood and Jack was in distress. This was one of the few occasions in my life that I prayed.

In readiness, a nurse ushered me into a recovery theatre which was bristling with resuscitation equipment and ventilators. I was surprised how quickly a small bundle was placed into my arms. I had a son! I was a dad! I was confused … elated … scared…

And so, on 18th June, along came Jack…. unenthusiastic and reluctant apparently and with a great deal of shouting, yanking and pulling (by the medical team). Because of the overly enthusiastic use of a vacuum extractor (I think the term is 'ventouse' rather than a Dyson), his head was bruised and misshapen. He looked like the love child of an ancient alien and Winston Churchill. Slowly, I then became aware that I was being watched, intensively. From the darkest corner of the room, I felt the glower of blood red eyes, the sound grinding teeth through a lipless orifice and the deafening sound of silence. Janet was far from happy that I had the bare faced nerve to hold the baby first.

After a week, Judith and Jack were allowed home. Despite the lack of an instruction manual, I took reasonably well to the feeding, cleaning and caring. I think I did OK but after another week went by, it was time to return to work and resume the job of keeping a roof over our heads.

While I was furiously working this meant, of course, that Judith was left at home with the baby and this was a concern under even normal circumstances. When she'd fallen pregnant, she told me that she'd stopped drinking for the sake of the baby. I had no reason to doubt her at that stage and she seemed to be sober, at least for the first few months. Also, fear not! The ever-present "in laws" took over and, God forgive me, I was actually grateful for their help. Little did I realise, that this was the start of their sinister iron like hold over their daughter, my son and even me. Inevitably, this would eventually result in the tearing apart of our family. Not only did the drinking 'start' again but it stepped up several gears.

From the moment I met Jack, my love for him was total and I looked forward, yearned even, for a happy and fulfilled family life. I couldn't have known of the psychotic obsession that Janet and Dick had for him.

They continued their overbearing presence in our lives. Their daily routine was to call Judith at around 630am every morning, arrive at around 8am, stay til around 7pm, then call again when they got home at around 815pm. This was every day – week in, week out including weekends – for the next 8 years. Their interference was suffocating to Judith. They controlled every aspect of her's and Jack's lives. They ran up huge heating bills (even in summer), abused the telephone and watched TV incessantly. Judith and the baby were taken out to the pub for lunches. It was a cycle of control, drinking and spending.

When Jack was around 6 months' old, we were invited to a former colleague's wedding in the home counties. We booked a hotel which was around 15 miles from the venue and drove down the previous day. At 7pm, I set him down to sleep. Judith was already face down on the bed, pissed. The wedding was an all-day affair the next day. Truthfully, it was far too long an experience for Jack but trying to prise Judith away from a booze fuelled party was about as easy as getting shit out of a rocking horse. I took Jack out of the evening session and did my best to entertain him in our 4 x 4 car, before settling him in his car seat to sleep. Eventually, the party began to break up at around 11pm. Judith eventually appeared at the door, hardly able to speak, never mind walk. I managed to bundle her into the car and we set off for our hotel. She collapsed against the window and snored loudly. Halfway there, then, she missed one of the pivotal moments of Jack's life. *"Mama ....*

Mama". She'd sacrificed hearing his first words for a skinful of booze!

On arriving at the hotel, I now had a difficult choice – who to carry in first? Because Jack was likely to be the better behaved and less trouble, I took him up to the room first and gently placed him in his crib, before rushing back down to the car. Anxious that I'd left Jack alone, I lifted Judith out and carried her to the room. I laid her on the bed and removed her shoes, before putting her handbag on the bedside drawers. With horror, I realised that the bag wasn't there! All our cards and all our money were missing. Without them, we couldn't check out and couldn't pay for fuel to get home. What was I going to do? If I went back to the wedding venue, would it be open? Would the bag be there? Should I take Jack and disturb him? What would happen if Judith awoke and found both of us missing? What if I left Jack and he needed attention which she couldn't give him? I decided on the lesser of the evils and abandoned them both. Rushing quickly back, I retrieved the handbag with great relief. In the morning, she could remember none of it but chose to tick me off for not waking her to hear his first words!

At home, because I was at work most of the time, to my eternal shame, I was slow to catch onto what was happening. To some extent, I was oblivious although there were bizarre clues to Dick and Janet's obsession with Jack. There were no less than 19 photographs of him around the house and, then, there was their ludicrous over-protection.

Jack was nearly a year old when I received a panicked call from Janet. She was in the car with Judith who was screaming and shouting erratically. Her foot was to the floor and she was weaving in and out of rush hour traffic like a maniac – horn blaring. Apparently, Janet had found an unusual mark which had appeared on Jack's head. He'd also gone limp. They were now headed for the GP's surgery at warp speed. I was instructed to get myself there – NOW! I dropped everything and got there sharpish. On being steered into the assessment room, I saw the pair of them crying in the corner and a nurse and a doctor looking at Jack's head in utter confusion. There was a perfectly circular, blueish red mark beneath his hair. I looked at Judith and Janet with utter contempt, licked my fingers, got a hold of Jack's head and rubbed the mark off! Embarrassed, I apologised to the doctor, explaining that Jack had been walking around the living room that morning, balancing a blackcurrant Fruit Shoot bottle on his head! Amusing this may be, but it was symptomatic of a destructive pattern of behaviour which would deliberately isolate Jack from me and the rest of my family.

His first birthday soon came around. He'd taken his first tentative steps two days earlier and Judith and her mother had decided to throw a huge party at our house. 40 attended, all but 3 being adults. It wasn't a celebration of his first 12 months rather than a demonstration of Judith and Janet's ability to organise alcohol fuelled binges. Most of the guests had a pleasant summer's day which started at 1pm and lasted well beyond 10pm and Jack's bedtime. They got increasingly pissed, to the point when Janet removed the palette from her mouth carrying her four front teeth and used it as a 'spoon' to scoop coleslaw into her dribbling disgusting gob. People began to leave.

It began to dawn on me that something was very wrong in the relationship between Judith and her parents. Jack was caught up in it too. When he was 18 months old, I'd suggested the three of us take a short break at Center Parcs, to get away from it all and have a well-earned rest. I gave Judith my credit card and asked her to arrange it. She booked a 3-bedroom lodge and, although I thought that was excessive, she told me it was the last accommodation remaining and had been reduced a lot in price. The evening before we were to travel, about three weeks later, Dick and Janet turned up at our house – suitcases packed! Needless to say, that they'd plotted to keep this from me, despite the fact that I'd paid for it all. It turned out to be an expensive and intensive experience!

One evening, we all went out for a meal. Judith and Janet had already 'tanked up' and were very drunk by the time we sat down. Judith was the worse for wear. She appeared to be 'sleep eating', eyes open but glazed, slurping gravy and peas off her knife and dribbling down her front. The sight of this made me feel sick and she was attracting the attention of other diners. Meanwhile, her parents seemed to pass it off as 'normal'. Jack started to cry so I reached out to lift him from his push chair. Dick snatched him away and thrust him towards Janet. I was furious but didn't want to cause a scene. Instead, I'd sort this out with Judith once she sobered up. Of course, she never did during the entire 3 days which followed.

A week later, Judith announced that she'd booked a "proper" holiday, being 7 days in Portugal. She'd paid for it on my credit card and I was furious. Besides, it was too soon to expose a toddler to an airflight and a hot climate. It was too late now, of course and, inevitably, Dick and Janet tagged along for the freebie. On the second day, disaster sprang. Dick was struck down with kidney stones. Whilst I did have sympathy for him because he was in agony, to make matters worse, the travel insurance we'd taken out had been suspended, supposedly because of a takeover. So, it was left to my trusty credit card to soak up the medicines and hospital bills which came to over £2,000. Daily taxi fares to the hospital racked up another £800. To add insult to injury, my card was compromised and some bastard in the USA added a further £250 to it! It would be another 2 years before the insurance eventually reimbursed me for the hospital fees. No word of thanks ever passed anyone's lips.

Back home, Judith's drinking was getting out of hand. She and Janet were using Jack like a puppet, and they knew exactly how to manipulate me. They even threatened to keep him away from me if I dared to expose him to my own family. It was a constant battle, and it took a toll on me. I was working over 60 hours a week, trying to build up and manage the business. At the same time, I was trying to keep up with their spending and demands and it was overwhelming. In private, I broke down at work on several occasions. I didn't have the energy, time, or reserves to fight off three control freaks and do everything else. Above all, I was terrified that Jack would get hurt or distressed.

The pattern of partying continued for the next six years, whether it be Christmas, BBQs, birthdays, the cats' birthdays .... any old excuse. As time went by, fewer and fewer of the regular people came as they began to realise the extent of Judith's problem and the control that Dick and Janet were exerting over her.

As Jack went through his pre-school years, Judith struck up 'friendships' with like-minded parents. I often returned from work to find a party in full swing with up to half a dozen kids and their mams and dads. My credit card continued to take the strain as the booze flowed freely. The thanks? On one occasion, a 'guest' threw up over my drive and van and, on another, I found one of the fathers lying drunk in the garden.

Because of my working hours, holidays were rare, but Jack did love Center Parcs. For his 6th birthday, I booked a break and Judith asked whether we could bring along a couple of his friends to keep him company, together with their mother. Unbeknown to me, she'd told the mother that there would be no need for her to pay because I was taking care of everything. They travelled over on the Friday morning and I joined them after work, on the Friday evening. Jack, his friends and I had a great time and I entertained them in a lot of activities over the next two days. My bond with Jack was growing ever stronger and when it was time for me to leave on the Sunday night, he presented me with two Center Parcs shopping trolley tokens. We had to rub each of them, swap them and, he kept one and I kept the other. When I got lonely, his instruction was that I should rub the token and that way, I'd remember him. He would do the same when he missed me. I left with tears rolling down my cheeks! I slept restlessly that night and Monday was difficult. I couldn't wait to see him again that evening, after they'd spent the final day there.

I got home early on Monday evening, but there was no sign of them. At 630, I called Judith. No answer. For the next 2 hours, I called again and again without any answer. By 10pm. I was getting really worried when the phone was answered by what appeared to be a gibbering idiot. It was Judith, pissed out of her skull. I asked her to pass the phone to Jack and only then did I find out what had happened. She'd driven them out of Center Parcs, straight to a 4-star hotel in Penrith. The kids had spent the best part of the day in the pool while the 2 mothers drank the day away. To make matters worse, she'd financed this junket on the company debit card. The £500 bill left me short to pay the VAT bill the following week. When she got home the following day, I vented my spleen at her. She was tearful and sorry … she hadn't meant to do it! But she didn't get it, she simply didn't understand the anguish and worry she'd caused. I'd had visions of my son lying splattered over some Cumbrian road, especially because of her drinking.

The merriment continued over the coming months. She frequently went to parties in the village, with Jack in tow. I would seek him and take him home at a reasonable hour, but she was now in the habit of staying out all night. One morning, at 5am, I found her drunkenly fumbling with the husband of one of her 'friends' on our own doorstep! I pulled her inside and she made a B line for Jack's bed, expecting to crawl in with him. The sight of what she'd just been doing and the prospect of her crawling into bed with Jack, disgusted me. I stopped her and, in the morning, she could remember nothing.

The late liquid lunches of Judith and her mother were a permanent feature of their lives. The behaviour and aggression which always followed were an acute embarrassment for us all. On one occasion, it erupted into a violent row with one of the other mothers in the school yard, with Janet screaming like a banshee. This sparked a flourish of complaints from other parents. Judith received a rebuke from the headmaster, not least because she'd now become a member of staff as a 'dinner nanny'. This was a role she'd use to stalk Jack around from school to school. The smothering continued ....

FOR BETTER OR WORSE

As the time approached for Jack to start school proper, it was decided that it would be best for him if his parents were married. I agreed for his sake and so it was that Judith and Janet took off to Edinburgh with Jack to plan the big day (including overnight stays, of course). The wedding would be attended by Judith's parents, Judith's brother and girlfriend, Judith's grandfather and Judith's friend, husband and son. It'd been made pretty clear that my family wouldn't be welcome, but I decided even not to ask them because of the contempt on both sides. I didn't want them or Jack upset. Janet had even told Jack that my mam wasn't his *"real"* grandma. Later, she came to be embarrassed by this when Jack cheerfully told me what she'd said.

The venue was an impressive "castle" hotel to the west of Edinburgh. The wedding party dispatched itself 2 days earlier – all that is, apart from myself and the old grandfather, who would be travelling with me, the evening before the ceremony. That way, I'd not be wasting more than a day off to get married. While I would be returning the following day, the rest of them would continue the festivities for a further 2 days. 5 days later, I was £5,000 more in debt and my shackles were even tighter.

Having arrived at the hotel around 8pm, I found that most of the guests were now blitzed. The notable exception was Judith's brother who spoke at great length about his parents, their drinking and the effect their behaviour had on him all his life. He'd even told them that they'd ruined his life but that simply resulted in them bad mouthing him. The parallels were startling.

Judith's grandfather was also a kindly old, retired gentleman miner. I had a lot of time for him but no more so than that evening. We'd made our excuses and headed off to our bedrooms, which were down a long flight of stairs. Roughly halfway down, we could hear a distinct rapid 'thudding' which grew progressively louder behind us. The staircase shook and, startled, we turned around, to be greeted by the sight of Janet sliding, feet first down the stairs, at an extremely unsafe speed. She'd obviously 'skidded' on the first step in her stocking feet, trying to go to the loo but was now shooting down, hitting her head on every step in the process. The old man quickly assessed the situation and gently steered me to the side so as not to impede Janet's progress and inevitable fate. He stared and gently shook his head as she hurtled past us.

That evening, alone in my prenuptial room, I contemplated the awfulness of my predicament. I didn't want to be here, I didn't want to marry Judith and I hated her parents. However, I'd willingly suffer all of it, for the sake of my son.

OF GERBILS, GIBBERISH AND GARBAGE

Shortly before her 39th birthday, Judith woke with a start from one of her binges. She'd been slumped in an armchair while Jack and I watched TV.

"I've done them …. I've done the three gerbils … I've done two gerbils and one ….."

Jack and I looked at one another. She sat there, wide-eyed, for a little while when he asked her what a gerbil was. She explained that it was a cross between a mouse and a hamster. Then, despite the early hour, she demanded that he went to bed with her, all the time talking about rodents. After they'd settled, he again asked what she'd been talking about. Then she turned on me. She hadn't mentioned anything about gerbils! … I was poisoning his mind against her! …. I was trying to get her to doubt her own sanity! Jack was frightened and reached for me, while I was standing there. She started to get even angrier and demanded I left them alone. As he clung to me, she was incensed. Over the next few minutes, as she began to lose consciousness once more, we gradually and quietly sneaked downstairs, leaving her to her poisoned farts and gerbils.

One late afternoon, in August that year, Jack called me while I was out and about, estimating. He wanted to adopt a younger sister! He was quite emotional and distressed. Obviously, he had no conception of what adoption was and I tried to tell him that this wasn't going to happen. I told him that I was happy with the son I had. However, he continued to plead and had it all worked out. We would move to a bigger house ... I wasn't too 'old' to adopt .... I was more intelligent than 'other' fathers ..... Of course, at such a young age, he couldn't have put all of this together. I was at a total loss to understand what she was thinking and why she was using him as a front for it all.

Judith's laziness extended to her housekeeping. Fortunately, I was brought up differently but, after a 10 – 12-hour shift, I hated nothing more than to come home to a pigsty and having to set about cleaning and tidying everywhere before making my evening meal. As Jack got older, the quantity and size of his toys grew beyond reason, thanks to the contributions from Dick and Janet. I started to feel like King Canute, trying to stop the tide coming in! The house regularly smelled and not only from cooking odours. As Judith's alcohol consumption spiralled, so did her tendency to order in vast quantities of kebabs which invariably ended up half eaten. The kitchen units were awash with grease and covered in dirty dishes, food waste, empty bottles and cat food.

The living room was equally disgusting …. Discarded clothing, more dirty dishes and partially consumed food, piles of ironing, crisp and biscuit packets, blackened upholstery from her boots …. and, of course, an abundance of empty bottles and cans. The heating and gas fire were at full tilt, no matter the weather, the TV and lights permanently on. The carpets were covered by ground in food, mud, cat shit and vomit. They also smelled of spilled alcohol. She'd even emptied the contents of her stomach in one patch and made no attempt to clean it up. Small animals and birds, both dead and alive, were ever present, courtesy of the cats.

The bathroom was strewn with dirty clothes, the bath was permanently filled with cold, scum tainted water and the toilet unflushed. Even the garage didn't escape with unused food from the freezer and fridge thrown onto the floor, despite the waste bin being close by. If I didn't clean it up, it would lie there, putrefying for days and even weeks.

Janet even had a go at her occasionally, for not pulling her weight. Her solution was to go around after me, undoing what I had cleaned and tidied. Eventually, I lost all heart and concentrated on the two rooms of the house I'd started to isolate myself to.

A CRY FOR HELP

A few weeks later, while lying in bed, Judith said she had something to tell me. She confessed that she was drinking in the mornings but that wasn't the worst of it. She was drinking while driving, with Jack in the car. I was shocked but, at least she'd admitted it. By admitting she had a problem, this could be a turning point! She genuinely seemed to want to change and I was going to do all I could to help. The decision to book a doctor's appointment was hers and she wanted me to be there with her. I listened as she described what she'd been doing. Her 'admission' to his question about how much she was drinking was 2 bottles of wine a day. He was very concerned and referred her to Alcoholics Anonymous (AA). At the time, neither he nor I realised what a vast understatement that was. Some 18 months later, I was counting up to 6 bottles of wine and 2 half bottles of vodka every day. This was a rate which would bring her to the point of death.

Judith contacted AA and we made arrangements to attend her first meeting at the local hospital. I was allowed to go with her for support but was sat at the back of the room. We were both made welcome, and, after tea and biscuits, the meeting got underway. There were 25 people, including

Judith, sitting in a circle. 3 people spoke and began with their name and *"... and I'm an alcoholic"*. The whole experience was a bit more evangelical than I'd expected and I was well out of my comfort zone. The stories they told were bizarre and shocking. There was the man who couldn't function without a glass in his hands, who woke up in his own shit and piss and often in lying in gutters. There were tales of families which had been torn apart. By far the most distressing account came from a respectably dressed, well-groomed middle-aged woman. A deputy head teacher, she'd thought that she'd hidden her addiction from her family by keeping her drinking for the bathroom and concealing bottles in linen cupboards, toilet cisterns and anywhere else she thought she'd get away with it. Her family knew, of course, to the extent where they were deeply traumatised and had eventually disowned her because of her behaviour and her risk to the children she was supposed to be responsible for.

I was determined that AA wasn't the place for Judith because, at this stage, neither she nor I were ready to admit that she was an alcoholic. She might have had a drink problem, but no way was she as bad as that! That was the level of Judith's deception and my naivety.

Over the coming months and years, I tried to get her help from a number of places. Of these, the longest term was the Northeast Council on Addictions in Gateshead (NECA). Judith was initially seen by a junior counsellor before being referred to higher levels as her addiction spiralled. As part of the process, was also allocated a therapist whose role was to support the family of addicts. Judith told me that she'd given 'level 3' authority to them, meaning that I would be given full access to her counsellor and kept informed. I hadn't asked for that, but as time went on, it was clear that the advice being given to me by my counsellor, Toni, was directly at odds with what Judith's advisor, Melissa, was giving her – or what Judith was telling me. I later found out that, in fact, Judith hadn't authorised Melissa to speak to me, give me any information about the programme or her progress. As a result, I only knew what Judith told me and she used 'Melissa' relentlessly in her attempts to manipulate me. Toni's advice to me was to stop Judith buying booze or stop helping her access it. Because I was at work most of the day, this effectively meant denying her any money. This only resulted in more rows and aggression and, in the end, it was Jack who again suffered as she ruthlessly used him as a weapon to get her way. I did set-up a separate bank account in my own name and channelled all the household expenditure through it, including food and clothing. Beyond that, though, Judith had access to our joint account where her salary was paid and, later, her benefits. I couldn't stop that but, because of her repeatedly going into the red and buying herself and Janet alcohol and pub meals, this was wiped out by bank charges. She then told me that Melissa had advised that she should drink all she wanted for the next 2 weeks and then reduce the vodka consumption before turning 'only' to wine. The suggestion was, if she stopped drinking suddenly, it could kill her. And so it was that I had to start giving her some money to put all this into effect. Besides, if she didn't have anything, our lives would have been utterly miserable.

A month later, she was still downing at least 3 bottles of wine a day, to my knowledge. Now, Melissa had told her that she must have money from me for the sake of her own independence and dignity. She was drinking because she was 'unhappy'. According to Judith, Melissa had been raised in similar circumstances and her father had been the source of the problem. Therefore, it was ME who was the problem and this was affecting Jack. It was ME who needed the treatment, because I was 'in denial'. Melissa also asked her why she stayed with me. Judith said it was because she had a 'nice house' and 'nice things'. Melissa snapped that she'd be better living in a cardboard box, with Jack, alone. She warned Judith that I would always blame her drinking 'for everything'. *"He would say that, wouldn't he!"*. Judith didn't need detox because her drinking was just a 'habit' and that wasn't the 'real' problem. I wasn't to try to speak to Melissa because she was 'too annoyed' with me. Judith had even called The Samaritans who'd told her to leave, with Jack.

Later that year, despite what Melissa had allegedly said, NECA offered Judith the chance to go into detox for 4 days. She was terribly distressed over this and didn't want to be apart from Jack for that length of time. However, she said she 'needed' to do it, although the offer was conditional on her appearing in front of a panel at 24/7, a specialist alcohol counselling service. A few days later, she told me that the offer had been withdrawn because she was still drinking too much. I called Toni to ask what was going on. After all, wasn't it their job to help stop the drinking? Unsurprisingly, it turned out that Judith hadn't been cooperating with them. She hadn't even been keeping appointments.

NECA was in Gateshead and 3 miles from home. Her meetings were on a Wednesday afternoon and Dick went along with her and sometimes, Janet would tag along. Dick refused to drive into Gateshead and, therefore, I had to finance the taxi fares in and out. One day, having some free time, I went into Gateshead to collect them. The hour's appointment passed and I waited. I waited for 2 more hours only to see the three of them, in my rear-view mirror, piling out of the pub next door. They'd nipped straight from counselling into the boozer! I felt betrayed and a gullible idiot.

At one point, NECA had asked to see Dick and Janet, alone. However, this wasn't because of their role in the drinking. It was because of the extreme pressure that Janet was putting on Judith to have Jack avoid all contact with my family and the stress it was causing her.

Judith's GP remained involved but not pro-active, apart from on one occasion. For this appointment, she'd asked me to go with her. On the morning, she'd tried to get out of bed but immediately collapsed. After a struggle, I got her there and listened as she complained of her shortness of breath, the lack of feeling in her legs and other symptoms of her excess drinking. I was stunned when she told him that she was drinking only 'a little more' than usual — perhaps a bottle or two of wine a day. He discussed the results of her recent blood tests. He obviously didn't believe her and said that she was 'knacking' her liver. Her gamma GT levels were at 380 and should be at only 40. He told her all her key indicators were well above the levels suffered by George Best, the recently deceased footballer before his liver transplant. He pointed out her bruising which was the result of the damage of her own liver. She started to cry and we went home but, later that day, I decided to call the doctor, from work. I knew of the patient confidentiality rules but I simply gave him the true scale of her drinking. He asked my permission to repeat this to her. *"What the hell"*, I thought *"Things can't get any worse!"* That afternoon, he hauled her back into the surgery on the pretense of more blood tests. He gave her 'both barrels' and bluntly told her she had a week to stop drinking or the situation would be irretrievable.

The doctor had called me to briefly outline what he'd told her. I was still at work but, when she got home, she called me in a blind rage. She'd denied everything I said, and the doctor now told her that her liver results had actually improved. On the way home, she therefore 'consoled' herself with another bottle of wine. She said that she'd called NECA and they'd told her that what I'd just done amounted to emotional blackmail and that I cared only for myself. Furthermore, because of what I'd done, Jack 'could be taken into care'. He was listening in to this 'conversation' and became terrified but Judith frequently used the threat of Jack being taken into care in front of him as a way of silencing me. I asked her when she was going to do something about her drinking. *"NEVER!"* was the reply. Not until people stopped 'nagging' her. I put the phone down.

The second intervention from a GP was soon afterwards when I visited the surgery because I was very unwell, not sleeping, no energy and no will. I summarised what my life was like and she diagnosed depression. Because of Jack being dragged into it all, she consulted with Judith's doctor and the pair of them decided to refer the matter to Social Services as a result of their concern for his welfare. Judith didn't know of this development at the time but sensed that the doctors weren't 'on her side'. She tried to discredit them in the family's eyes, having called NHS Direct one night to discuss her badly numbed and tingling legs. After the call, she claimed that they'd told her to stop seeing her GP because he was 'blinkered' and her problems were nothing to do with alcohol.

Later that year, Judith was referred to a liver

specialist at the Nuffield Hospital in Newcastle. She drank on the way there and drank in the waiting room. As usual, in public, this was out of a pop bottle containing just enough of the soft drink to disguise the vodka. She was eventually offered a six-week residential detox programme. Again, she initially accepted only to turn it down because she didn't want to be away from Jack. She tried to fob me off saying that she'd arrange something with NECA instead. Not only was that a lie but I later found a letter from 24/7 concealed under magazines, in the bidet. She'd missed her appointment with them and wouldn't be offered another chance at detox until she called them to explain why. When I confronted her, she flew into another fury and tore up the letter.

I'd even sought help from RELATE marriage counselling and spent a full course with them. Judith didn't know and would have been furious. However, I was desperately searching for answers to our predicament. Sadly, they concluded that the marriage was dead. They were very concerned for Jack and warned me that they were inclined to report the situation to Social Services. They were also concerned for my own mental and physical health. It was only by telling them that the GPs had already referred the matter that they didn't act.

With the benefit of hindsight, I was obviously experiencing depression. I was racked with physical pain all over my body and my memory was shocking. I had to write everything down and began to keep a journal. While I refused medication, I did accept counselling with the practice. Over the months I saw them, they also concluded that the marriage was dead and had concerns for Jack. They forced me to confront the situation with him – how was I going to protect him and how would I care for him when I ended the marriage? I was under real pressure now and agreed to speak directly to Social Services. When I did, the response was totally hostile.

A SLAVE TO THE SAUCE

Her drinking was now an all-day habit, starting at 815am with a trip to the off-licence. She'd wait outside until it opened and then compete with the hordes of kids buying their crisps and sweets on their way to school. Later, as she became an increasing danger and incapable, I'd find myself brow beaten, bullied, cajoled and threatened into doing that early shift for her. I was deeply ashamed and embarrassed, but this was the only way I could keep a lid on her rage and the effect that had on Jack. Better to keep her pissed than angry.

If she was planning a day out, she'd also buy several small bottles of pop so she could empty most of the contents and top them up with vodka. These bottles were her constant companions. I've found that alcoholics believe that vodka has no smell and gives them the instant 'hit' they need. In truth, it does smell and everyone else can detect the foul stench oozing out of their pores, even at some distance.

Often in the afternoons or school holidays, Jack would discover that his mother had gone missing. He knew he could find her though – in the garage, trying to keep her secret away from him and, bizarrely, her own mother who was the major cause of her drinking problem. Having drank herself into a stupor, she'd then insist that he went to bed with her. In this way, a great deal of his early life was spent in bed or under a duvet in the living room, at all times of day and in all weathers with her invariably naked, except for a pair of panties.

Judith was still working as a 'dinner nanny' at Jack's school and she tried to persuade me that he was unhappy there, being often bullied. I asked him and he confirmed it, although I couldn't help but feel that he'd been rehearsed. This followed the violent argument in the school yard involving another mother, Judith and Janet. I suspected this might have more to do with saving their faces. However, because Judith and Jack had fallen in with a couple of pretty obnoxious families, I went along with the idea that he should be moved and wrote to my old primary school in Whickham, asking whether there could be a place for him. So, his education was disrupted at the age of six and he entered Whickham Parochial Church of England School. Judith gave up her position at his old school but to my astonishment and after her considerable efforts, she managed to land the same role at his new school! She simply couldn't be away from him.

Judith's new job suited her and her mother perfectly. After work, they could drink away the afternoons, often in the pub next to the school. I was furious, when I found out and tried to reason with her. Eventually, she proposed a new 'drinking plan' where there would be no alcohol after 2pm on the day before school. This, of course, was complete bollocks. At this stage, she was downing 4 bottles of wine and half a bottle of vodka a day during the week. She could guzzle a bottle of wine in 15 minutes and the money was hemorrhaging. In the glove box of her car, she kept extra strong mints, toothpaste and mouthwash, along with the empty vodka bottles. It was clear that she was now drinking AT school and doing her utmost to hide it. However, I was keeping in close contact with the head teacher and, one day, he told me that he'd had complaints from other members of staff about Judith's 'smell' and behaviour. He was very concerned but couldn't do anything about it unless he caught her 'in the act'. He, personally, suffered from a loss of sense of smell and, without that, a key part of the evidence was 'hearsay'. Instead, he had to settle for 'counselling' her after taking advice from the HR department of the local education authority. No direct action was ever taken against her.

Through-the-night drinking completed the 24-hour alcohol cycle. She frequently woke me to demand more drink, or that I sit with her while she binged on it. I was absolutely knackered, and it was taking a toll on Jack too because she slept in his bed and he was woken up several times every night.

On the eve of her 38th birthday, she had again 'celebrated' with Dick and Janet that afternoon. After they'd gone home, she had a panic attack and wheezed badly as she tried to breathe. Jack was alone with her and he was absolutely terrified. He called me and I rushed home, only to find her face down on the floor, arse in the air and snoring loudly. Resisting the temptation to kick her raised posterior, I instead settled Jack, made his tea and we watched TV together until his bedtime. By now he was so used to adult company in bed that he didn't want to be alone. I lay on top of the duvet alongside him. I told him made up stories, which he enjoyed and, after a while, we both fell asleep. At around 2am, Judith woke us, switching on all the lights, demanding that we sing 'Happy Birthday' and join her in a drink. I told her there was no booze and I wasn't going to get any at that time of the morning. She screamed a tirade of abuse at me and told Jack that we were going to 'split-up', much to his distress.

Night drinking left us at our most helpless and anxious, especially when she mixed the vodka with diazepam and citalopram. Then, we would have the added worry of visions, usually involving monkeys climbing through the window. Even though he couldn't see them, Jack was scared and became less and less inclined to be alone with her.

The mornings were hell, especially if she'd hadn't been able to satisfy her cravings during the night. She couldn't recall what had happened the previous day, she shook, sweated, shivered and vomited. Then there was the paranoia and aggression. She couldn't eat, make Jack's breakfast or even put up his lunch. She could do nothing around the house. There came a point where I decided to disable the car engine to stop her driving. I also lodged the garage door into place so it couldn't be opened. Dick, I thought, could take her to work, but as he did, she called at the local COOP where she bought silly things... and of course, a bottle of vodka.

The amount of money being spent on booze was rocketing. In the later stages, I calculated that it was around £150 a week – and that was just the stuff I knew about. Then there was what she was buying Dick and Janet and the daily meals out or ordered in. The drain on the cash in the business was extremely serious and then, I became aware that she was hammering credit cards.

Before I set up the separate account for

household spending, the direct debits on our joint account were forever being bounced for lack of funds and the bank charges were obscene. I blocked her access to the business accounts and transferred credit card balances to interest free options, cutting up the old cards in the process. She still had access to the joint account for her own needs and the new account effectively became the main household account, under my control. By now she was no longer employed in the business, so her income was from Jack's child benefit, tax credits and £50 cash a day from me. I bought all the groceries and, this way, I was able to ensure that Jack would be properly fed and not 'second fiddle' to the booze shopping.

The £50 a day I gave her was never enough. It was meant to be for essentials but, of course, much of it always ended up in the off licence, or in her parents' pockets. She was also in the habit of buying Jack 'presents' on a daily basis. This was to compensate him for what she knew was the desperately distressing and sad situation he was in. So, whenever I criticized her spending, she would turn to him and say to him that I was 'telling her off' for getting him this or that. It was just another use of my son as a weapon.

During school holidays, I gave her extra to

entertain Jack. I also gave Jack his own money. When she'd spent her money in the off licence in the morning, she came back for more in the afternoon. If I refused, she'd simply take Jack's but he still ended up being taken nowhere. If I agreed and told Jack that I wanted to hear all about his day when I got back, I was accused by both Judith and Janet of being a control freak and playing 'mind games'. Often, Jack's money box was raided. I regularly returned from work to find Jack, and any friend he had with him, hungry. So, I fed them or took them to McDonalds or the local fish and chip shop when I was too tired to cook. Once, when we returned from McDonalds, Janet called to ask Judith what she'd been doing with him later that day. Judith was so drunk that she couldn't recall anything – even that Jack and I had just been to McDonalds. She asked Jack to tell his grandmother what they'd done that afternoon. He knew that she'd be in deep trouble if he told the truth, so he instinctively said, *"the pictures"*.

She was going to the local Marriott hotel, which was less than a mile away, more and more often. Eventually, she pushed me to enroll her in the Health and Fitness Club so that they could use the pool. It was £57 a month and I told her we couldn't afford it. She countered that, unless I did, she'd make no efforts to get better or go into detox. So,

I agreed to go along with it and she joined, with the ever-present Janet free loading on the back of the membership. Together, the pair of them stayed dry, propping up the bar and leaving Jack to his own devices for hours, in the pool. Despite the short distance, they took taxis to and from the place – and everywhere else as it happens. She thought nothing of paying £13 for taxis to take Jack for a £1.99 happy meal from McDonalds. She took taxis to the supermarket, off licence … anywhere and everywhere.

Her spending was prolific. One August day she received a £380 tax rebate. Two days later only £40 was left and she was demanding more. She would often run the joint account into overdraft buying a £3.99 half bottle of vodka resulting in £90 bank charges. The home heating and lighting bills were astronomically high with summer bills as much as £700 a month as the three of them sat watching TV with curtains closed, gas fire blazing and central heating blasting out.

One day, I hit on the idea of giving her another £100, which I'd top up when she gave me receipts. This made me as popular as a dog with rabies, not least with Janet and Dick. The reason – I hadn't been aware of the amount of money she was simply handing over to them. The first time I gave her the extra £100, she had £40 left at the end of the day. She said she'd bought groceries, which was a lie because I'd just brought the groceries the previous evening. At this point, she threatened to leave with Jack and get a council house.

BOOZE AND BLUE LIGHTS

Judith was now having difficulty breathing, describing it as not being able to fill her lungs with sufficient air. She complained of a lump in her throat and a blockage in her windpipe, resulting in her aimlessly and frantically walking around the house with a finger on her throat. She anxiously wafted air into her face with her other hand. She had large quantities of asthma inhalers but continually called NHS Direct for help. Over the next 2 years, the sight of paramedics at our house was routine, one week as many as 3 separate occasions. Each time, they'd ask her if she'd been drinking and her response was she'd 'had a few'. One female paramedic even passed comment about the amount of empty bottles lying around the place. She was regularly diagnosed as having a 'panic attack' and one medic even gave her a paper bag to breathe into. The truth was, however, that her liver was growing ever larger and pressing onto her diaphragm, stopping her lungs operating to their fullest extent. Nevertheless, the visits from the emergency services became something of a ritual.

One Friday afternoon, shortly before Jack's seventh birthday, I followed an ambulance containing Judith, leaving Jack in the care of Dick. At the hospital, she was kept in a quiet room until she calmed down. Because we were likely to be some time, she asked me to call Dick and to have him take Jack to their house. I'd previously spoken to NECA and now told her that I was going to restrict her vodka to 200cl in the morning and 200cl in the evening. *"Fine"* she said before telling me that she'd get more from 'somewhere else'. A doctor eventually arrived and asked if she was OK with me being in the room. Judith agreed before the doctor questioned her on her general health and then coming to the question of alcohol. Once again, she deliberately hid how much she was drinking and became annoyed when I contradicted her. She was given a course of diazepam to last the weekend and the doctor insisted she saw her GP on Monday and that she should fully cooperate with NECA. She was warned not to drink while taking the meds. We discussed the 'blockage' in her throat, but the doctor assured us that there was nothing there. I said that Judith wasn't getting enough support and repeated what her GP had said about her excessive use of alcohol, the situation now approaching critical. When I described the aggression and physical attacks, Judith swore at me, calling me 'pathetic' and accusing me of wanting her to be 'committed' so that I could 'take Jack'. Nevertheless, she was discharged and we went off to the hospital pharmacy for her diazepam. On the way, she told me that, if it wasn't for Jack, she'd kill herself. As we travelled home, she had me stop at an off-licence.

I went back to work at 5pm, returning at 7pm. She was drunk again, having got through nearly a full bottle. Dick was still at our house with Jack because Judith felt she needed him there. After he left, she took 2 diazepam rather than the one she'd been prescribed. She refused to go to bed and quickly became stupefied in front of the TV. Three times around 8pm, she asked Jack if he wanted to go swimming. He reacted fairly angrily when she then started to go on about swimming in the neighbour's pond because 'the cats had eaten all the fish'. I told Jack not to answer as she got louder. She gulped the rest of her wine before pouring another glass and staggering to the dining room where we had a sofa bed, demanding that he went with her to sleep.

On Monday, I took her to the doctors' where she was prescribed an increased dose of citalopram and stronger blood pressure medication to treat her. very high hypertension. On the way home, she stopped off for a bottle of vodka.

I dropped her at home and went off to get her prescriptions. When I got back, she was pissed. Dick told me that NECA had called and asked to see her immediately. I managed to get her into the car and took her over, although I wasn't allowed in with her. When she emerged, she told me that they'd offered to refer her to a more specialist counsellor. Until then, she was to drink 'normally' and also see a marriage guidance counsellor, which they could arrange. On the way home, she bought another bottle of vodka.

I eventually managed to get to work at around 3pm for a couple of hours. When I got back, Dick told me she'd taken her meds and gone to bed in the dining room. She wanted Jack to stay at theirs. I wasn't happy about it but I thought it might be best for his sake that evening. I called Toni at NECA and, predictably, everything Judith had told me about her meeting was crap. She heard me speaking to Toni and became aggressive because of her paranoia. She got up and worked her way through another bottle of vodka and got gradually incoherent. She said she needed to *"go somewhere"*, meaning rehab. With that she went back to bed with the rest of the vodka and was kept company by the monkeys coming through the window.

The following day, she decided to go to her parents' for a few days. I dropped her off and Jack came back with me. We lived peacefully for those days and I fed him, clothed him, took him to school, collected him and entertained him. It was enjoyable, normal family life. Then, a few days later, just before collecting Jack from school, Janet called me to say that Judith was having another 'attack'. Dick was on his way to the shop to get her some vodka but when Jack and I arrived, she was 'feeling better'. After a while, we left, only to be called back by Dick. She'd suddenly got worse and they'd called an ambulance. When we got there, she refused to let me go with her and this caused some concern among the paramedics. I could feel an air of suspicion towards me and, once again, Jack watched all of this.

I left him with Dick and took Janet with me to the hospital. She'd tried to stop me talking about Judith's drinking in front of the paramedics, so I asked her directly how much she'd had. She was deliberately vague but did say she'd had a couple of 'small' bottles of vodka. Dick later let it slip that she and Judith had polished off a full bottle between them.

We got to the hospital and rushed straight to A&E only to see Judith standing, relatively upright and laughing. She was drunk of course but had discharged herself rather than suffer a three-hour wait. I asked her if she realised just how much all of this was affecting Jack. I suggested he spend a few more days with me but both Judith and Janet didn't want him to and Janet became quite aggressive, asserting that he'd be 'fine' with them. Again, I didn't want to fight in front of him and reluctantly went along with it.

At 3am in the morning, Judith called me at home. She was having another 'episode'. I told her to use the paper bag and stay calm. At 430am, Janet rang – she'd called yet another ambulance. Judith was going to hospital and, when she'd been discharged, they were all coming down in the morning so that she could see her own GP.

At 0830am, I called the surgery to book an appointment for her, I explained that she was alcohol dependent, vulnerable and at risk. It was arranged for the doctor to call her after she got home. When she arrived, she wasn't pleased at what I'd done. There was nothing wrong with her – all she needed was more vodka. I told her the price would be cooperation with the doctor and she agreed.

Things settled down over the next 48 hours. Then she woke me at 10pm, having called another ambulance. Jack was still asleep and Dick and Janet were tucked up in their own beds in Northumberland. I called my elderly parents who agreed to come and babysit. After she left in the ambulance, I followed to the hospital and, again, when I got there around 45 minutes later, there was Judith discharging herself. She wasn't going to wait to be seen3 weeks of hospital free incidents followed. However, one June day, Janet called me to say that they were taking Judith to hospital because her blood pressure was very low. I asked my parents to collect Jack from school and worked on until 5pm before leaving for the hospital. Judith was on a drip and she kept squeezing the bag so as to finish quickly and be discharged. She then sent me to collect Jack because she and Janet didn't want him left with my parents. Jack, however, had asked them for roast chicken, mash and veg. Mam, dad and he went out to buy the ingredients and he wasn't about to be hurried. Judith, Dick and Janet got home at 630pm and endlessly hassled me to get him home because Janet and Dick wanted to see him. We finally arrived at 730pm, much to their frustration.

FIGHTING BACK AGAINST THE ODDS

Judith continued to deny the extent of her drinking, especially to herself. Time and again, I'd talk to her about what *could be,* what she could do with her life, the possibility of developing her interest in children into a career ....

Throughout, I helped her arrange and keep her medical appointments, helped her in and out of the bath when her legs wouldn't function or she was too pissed to stand. I looked after the house, cleaned, tidied, ironed and shopped. I fed, cared for and entertained Jack and I worked long and hard to keep a roof over our heads. This was me doing my bit to keep the household and family functioning as well as possible, this was me being a father. Then, to be constantly accused by Judith and her parents of playing no part in Jack's upbringing was an outrage. Later, to be asked by Social Services why I was 'complaining' about the woman who'd 'brought up' my son was breathtakingly sexist and prejudiced! The woman couldn't look after herself, let alone, Jack. She was either asleep, couldn't be bothered or couldn't move. Her idea of looking after Jack was to take him to bed with her or shove him under a quilt in the living room to watch TV. She didn't stimulate or entertain him or take him anywhere. The only places she or they regularly took him were to pubs or to the Marriott hotel pool. We had a perfectly good public pool less than 100 yards from the house. Unfortunately, it lacked one essential facility – a bar. Jack protested about having to go to the hotel and was deeply unhappy about being left on his own while his mother and grandmother plonked themselves in the lounge bar. The pool was used by 'old people' and businessmen when he could be having a good time with his friends at the local baths. When he said these things, he was quickly slapped down.

I was forced to accept that the stories I'd heard at Alcoholics Anonymous were also typical of Judith. Her personal hygiene deteriorated. Once such an attractive, proud and intelligent girl, she now smelled and not only of booze. She rarely washed or bathed on her own accord. She would bleed from every orifice, bruise terribly over her entire body and yet resist going to the doctors. Her alcohol fuelled cravings for kebabs resulted in a putrid smell coming from her pores, hanging on her clothes and in her hair. She would rather spend money on booze than food. She would go to bed pissed and hungry, getting increasingly depressed, She'd sleep most of the day and vomit over herself or over dishes in the sink rather than use the toilet. All of this was left for me to clean up. As the nerves in her feet degraded, they turned black and the smell was awful. Sometimes, she'd resort to crawling around on all fours, usually to get at more drink. While she didn't gain weight, her body shape changed to copy her mother. Her upper stomach bloated as her liver grew ever larger. When I changed the bedding, the mattress was usually covered in urine stains. I thought that this was limited to her sleeping but, one evening at Jack's rugby club presentation, I noticed that her seat and back of her dress were drenched in piss. It was left to me to get her medications but then she'd deliberately avoid taking them. She frequently missed her appointments with NECA, the hospital and even the benefits office. Our lives were out of control but I was now determined to fight back!

The first thing I did was to approach the neighbours to ask them not to offer her with drink when she paid them 'social calls'. Up to now, I'd kept our 'problem' secret because I was ashamed. Now, I found that talking helped. They were shocked but also very supportive.

I'd already taken control of the family finances. I'd also taken Judith out of the business and stopped Dick working there for an hour a day and being paid for a week. There was now no way that money could be filtered through to the in-laws except by bits and pieces coming from what I gave Judith.

Next came the supply of booze. It would be dangerous for me to suddenly cut this off. Everyone had told me this. Instead, I began to buy it myself to control the flow. At first, I bought 3 bottles of wine a day and allowed her to have one bottle at a time. Vodka was for emergencies and to be used only when she urgently needed a hit. Soon, though, she began to experience withdrawal as the effects of the wine diminished. The vodka had to be used as a way of controlling her cravings and aggression. I bought the cheapest possible ½ bottles and kept them in the van. I siphoned off 1/3 and topped the bottle up with water. Even then, I allowed her the bottle only when the withdrawal was horrendous and disturbing. Eventually, my little deception was rumbled as she was no longer satisfied. So, I stopped watering it down and stocked up with a few bottles to keep in the van to save repeated trips to the off licence. Whenever she demanded a new bottle, I got into the van, drove around the corner, parked up for a while before returning with a bottle in my hand. If she knew that I was carrying stock, she would have finished it all and then some. If the family had consisted only of me and

her, I would have refused point blank to play ball. In fact, the marriage would have been over long before now. However, the supply of alcohol was the only way I could manage her moods and temper. Without it, Jack's life, and my own, were a living hell.

Early one morning, after Jack had gone off to stay with Dick and Janet the evening before, Judith got out of bed to look for a drink. Suddenly, there was a piercing scream. I rushed to the stair head to find her lying at the bottom, She'd slipped and badly hurt her ankle, but that wasn't the cause of her agony. She had the screaming heebee geebes because she hadn't been able to find any booze. She demanded, pleaded for it. I decided that this had to be a turning point, now that Jack was out of the house. I went to the van and brought in a bottle. I put her in an armchair. On the coffee table in front of her, I placed the bottle alongside a photograph of Jack. *"YOU CHOOSE!"*, I demanded. That little boy needed his mam, wanted his mam and his life was in tatters because of her drinking. *"YOU CHOOSE!"*. She sobbed in anguish for 5 minutes before reaching for the bottle and limping back off to bed in silence.

The opening battle in the booze war had been lost.

THE FIFTH COLUMN

My war against the bottle wasn't going well, the campaign being seriously undermined by the 'Fifth Columnists', Dick and Janet, whose role was central and at the heart of the problem. Their philosophy was simple. Life was about having fun ... and you can't have fun without drinking! Everything took second place. I remember that I was very ill one Christmas having caught an acute case of bronchitis. I'd taken to my bed and stayed there for several days, uninterrupted by the three of them. For New Year's Eve, Judith had arranged for them all to go to a friend's house for a party. Janet persuaded her and Dick, along with Jack, to go on ahead so that she could wash the dinner dishes. I remember lying shivering and sweating when, suddenly, I was drenched in ice cold water. Janet had thrown the entire contents of a bucket over me. *"That's for not having fun!"* she cackled before drunkenly stumbling out of the front door.

The following New Year, I got home early from work, looking forward to spending the rest of the day and New Year's Day with Jack. As I parked on drive, the house was in unusual darkness. In the kitchen, I was met by a note from Judith, telling me that Dick and Janet had decided that they should all spend New Year at their house. And so, it was an especially lonely and depressing New Year and I went to bed at 1030pm. At around midnight, though, I was awakened by a phone call from Janet, begging me to come and collect Judith (not Jack) because she was 'out of control'. I didn't want to see the drunken bitch and saw this as poetic justice for Janet. Rather than openly refuse, I came up with an outstanding excuse …..I couldn't … because I'd been drinking.

On New Year's Day, they demanded that I come and collect her. By this time, though, my parents, having taken pity on me, had invited me for lunch. I said that I was going out for a meal and would pick Judith up later. This was greeted by howls of fury and me being accused of 'not caring'. They even had Jack call me to voice his own anger. Later that day, Dick brought both him and Judith home and that's when I learned the truth, from Jack. The previous evening, Judith and her parents had been drinking heavily when Judith and Janet had begun to argue and trade physical blows between them. Dick had tried to prise them apart and Jack had become very frightened and distressed. Some neighbours had heard the racket and come into the house. They tried to comfort Jack and told him that he should run to them if the violence blew up again.

Dick was a drinker but didn't abuse it to the

extent that Janet and Judith did. In fact, as Judith's alcoholism worsened, he seemed to drink less. To an extent, he became a steadying influence and I believed that Jack may be safe in his hands, when he was kept away from me. However, he was very much afraid of Janet, who dominated him, but also very close to Judith, although not close enough to face up to her problem. He lacked the courage to try to break the harmful influence of his wife, despite often threatening to leave her. Judith was also terrified of Janet. She drank more whenever Janet called her and less when she wasn't around.

Both Dick and Janet tried to disguise the extent of Judith's (and their own) drinking. Dick would take empties to as many bottle banks as were needed to get rid of them, because our recycle bin would be overflowing after a couple of days of being emptied. He would also conduct 'hunts' around the house to collect up the hidden cans and bottles because he knew where the 'hidey holes' were .... inside washing powder boxes, behind the fridge or freezer, behind the washing machine, inside toy boxes, in the loft, in the garden, on top of kitchen cabinets, inside kitchen cabinets, inside radiator cabinets, under Jack's bed . . . .

INNOCENT CASUALTIES OF WAR

Judith needed to be surrounded by children. It wasn't uncommon for there to be up to 6 of them in our house at any time, but especially in the evenings when I got back from work. Some of them were kids she'd just met on the street and Jack didn't know who they were. There was probably a practical reason for this and that was that she wouldn't feel guilty about leaving Jack alone when she fell asleep. There was another reason, though. Despite being in her late thirties, Judith hadn't matured beyond the mindset of a teenager and that was down to Janet's iron control over her. She was never allowed or encouraged to develop as an individual. Judith was ONE of the kids. She was in her comfort zone.

The house was a disaster zone. It was commonly trashed with food and mud ground into the carpets, potato pellets stuck to the walls and smashed glass on the floor. I often found the kids trampolining in the rain or camping in soaking wet tents outside. All the while, Judith was unconscious in a chair or getting pissed with other parents. The lack of care and supervision was an accident waiting to happen. And so it was, for example, that one of Jack's young friends suffered a broken arm. Fortunately, I'd just returned from work and was able to whip the child up to A&E, while Judith continued to party with the parents who then became sober to suggest that they were going to sue.

The kids would stay over until around 8pm. Then the curse of the sleepovers started, actively encouraged by Janet. My house was no longer my own and I began to live in my study. If I wasn't around, the children often went unfed. At bedtime, she bundled up to 3 of them in the sofa bed in the dining room, before crawling, drunk, in with them. The subject of her drinking was an open topic for discussion and the more sensitive of them would ask to be taken home. More often than not, though, it was a blast and they got away with things they never could in their own homes. Before they went to sleep, Judith would put 18 certificate movies on the TV for them to watch. They laughed at the offensive comments made about me by her and her mother. There was no respect and two of the little angels even threatened to 'smash my face in' for 'not having fun. Wonder where that came from!

One of Jack's young friends was at our house morning, noon and night continuously, for weeks. It was obvious that his parents were in no mood to have him at home, particularly during school holidays. I often tried to return him, only to find that they had just 'gone out', sometimes as late as 10pm. So, we continued to feed and house him, even buying clothes as he'd arrive without a change. One day, Judith announced that he had ringworm and, not only did she not arrange for him to go home, but unknown to me, she allowed him to share Jack's bed! When Jack then developed a rash, I was furious. She clearly knew the risk that she'd exposed him to. She promised to take him to the GP the following day but didn't. By this time, I was livid, so she faithfully promised to do it the following day. Again, she didn't. telling me that the surgery had been shut all day. Why was she avoiding taking him? So, on the third day, I called from work to find out what the doctor had said, only to discover that Dick and Janet had taken them both to the pub instead! Jack later told me that his rash had gone without having to see the doctor. He also said that he hadn't wanted to go to the pub, but they'd threatened to leave him at home, alone if he didn't come along with his friend.

Jack's young pal stayed with us for the entire summer holiday. Then, one day, while Jack and he were playing in the garden and the 3 adults were entertaining themselves in the usual way, the young lad collapsed. He was in a lot of pain and distress and his lips had turned blue. Judith and Janet were hysterical. I rushed home to find that, at least, his parents had taken him to hospital, since Dick couldn't. It turned out that he had a congenital heart issue which they'd known all about but hadn't told us. So, he hadn't had a heart attack, but his condition was serious enough for the hospital to want to see him. When I got back from work again, at 8pm, I was shocked to see that his parents had again dumped him at our house! After the holidays, Jack and the boy returned to their respective schools and I later found out that his school nurse had reported the situation to the head teacher and there'd been some sort of enquiry, which resulted in the school advising his parents to keep him away from Judith and Jack.

As word spread of Judith's behaviour, there was a noticeable tail-off in the number of children visiting our house, so Judith fell back on using the Marriott hotel. Even there, on one occasion, she was dragged out of the bar by a lifeguard. She'd left Jack and her own young cousin in the pool for 2 hours and the other child had hurt his foot. Jack had to ask for help, because he couldn't find his mother.

There had been no more worrying aspect to Judith's drinking than her driving under the influence. After she'd admitted this to me and before I'd disabled the car, I'd begged her to stop. She'd said that she would and I'd foolishly believed her. The car continued to be parked bizarrely on the drive or on the road. There were a number of close shaves and, one morning she'd been 'pulled' by the police having just come out of the off-licence. Fortunately, the officer only wanted to 'advise' her of some excess wear on the outside of a tyre. To this day, I can't understand how she got away with it. At the height, she was driving all over the place .. to the off-licence, to work, to the pub, to take Jack to school, to ferry him and his friends around. When I became aware of the fact that she'd broken her promise, I threatened to report her to the police. Instead, it was in August of that year, that I disconnected the spark plugs and removed the rotor arm from the car engine. I also wedged the garage door shut.

Later that day, before leaving work, I called home to ask if they needed anything from the shops. Jack said they did need a few things but that his mam hadn't been able to start the car. He asked if I knew anything about it. She always insisted that he repeated aloud, anything I said to him on the phone. When I told him what I'd done and why, she went berserk and started smashing the house up, much to Jack's horror. She accused me of 'grinding' her down and taking her freedom away. Dick wasn't happy either. He'd earlier tried to force open the garage door because he wasn't going to drive her around. When I got home, she raged against me and wished me dead, in front of Jack. He ran out and I followed him. Comforting him on the front steps, he then said something which has lived with me ever since. It tore my guts out when he said, *"Dad, I don't have a very nice life"*.

I left the car at the house when we eventually split. One day, though, on delivering the week's groceries, I was mystified to find it outside, on the road. My curiosity turned to dread when I saw that the nearside had been completely trashed. It looked as though it had been crashed and lying on its side. It was scraped from front to back, the passenger door was dented, the door handles and wheel trims were missing, the indicators were gone, the wheels were buckled and the bumper was broken Fortunately, they were OK but she tried to tell me that it had been hit in the street by a milk float. The truth was somewhat stranger as you'll read later. Meanwhile, I was £3,000 poorer.

PURRFECT MADNESS AND OBSCENITIES

Her general behaviour became increasingly bizarre.

We'd already had a discussion about her filling the house with kids and the risk of it all because she couldn't look after them. There'd been a couple of times when she rightly refused Jack's pestering to have someone sleepover. The problem was that, if I supported her, she'd change her mind. She wanted to be seen to be on the 'other side', especially in front of him so she could turn around and accuse me of stopping him from 'having fun' because I 'wouldn't allow it'. On one occasion and in front of Jack and a friend, she demanded that I took the three of them to the Marriot hotel so they could stay the night. Apart from the stupidity of it all, I couldn't afford it and told her so. The kids started to talk about her being drunk and Jack's friend even disappeared into the garage and came back waving an empty bottle of wine to show me. By this time, Judith had gone into the dining room. She called for Jack and had him come back to me saying that I'd stolen her money and that I had to 'give it back' so she could pay for the hotel. At this time, my dad was helping me remodel our front garden. Because the whole thing was becoming very heated, I suggested he leave. He did and also took Jack's friend back to his own home. Judith then tore out of the house and banged on several of the neighbours' doors to tell them what a bastard I was. When she came back, she found me calling Dick and Janet to tell them what was going on. She grabbed the phone and tore it out of the wall before doing the same to the two extensions in the house. At the sight of this, Jack was extremely upset. Shortly afterwards, Dick and Janet arrived. Dick tried to calm Judith while a very drunk Janet found me in the study, comforting Jack. She launched into an outburst of abuse against **my** mother, accusing her of being the cause of Judith's drinking! I hadn't a clue what she was talking about until a bizarre story unfolded.

Some months earlier, Judith had mentioned to my mother that she couldn't get our clothes fully clean in the washing machine. I admit that mam did have an acidly sharp sense of humour and she quipped *"It's not the machine, dear, it's the user!"*. According to Janet, this traumatised Judith so much that she'd turned to drink. By now, I'd had enough and bluntly told Janet that SHE was the cause of Judith's drinking and their inability to 'have a good time without booze'! The balloon went up! Janet tore out of the room screaming at Dick and Judith, telling them what I'd said. The three of them stormed into the study, yelling at me in front of Jack. He was in my arms, sobbing and trembling as I covered him while Judith set about me with all her strength. He was hot with sheer terror while I tried to tell him that everything was going to be OK but that day broke me. I was so ashamed that I openly cried in front of him. Eventually Judith suffered another 'panic attack' and wasn't able to breathe. I called the paramedics and the three of them left for hospital again. Jack wanted to sleep with me that night but, on her return, Judith stopped that. At 2 am, I was wakened by him slipping in with me. He was feeling sick and cuddling into me. No bloody wonder, poor kid!

Judith was also getting very confused. I came into work one morning to see the answerphone light flashing, as was often the case when customers called out of hours. There was just one message ... a very long one. It was Judith, having a full-blown row with the machine because it wasn't answering her questions. She'd called in between the time I'd left home and before I got to the workshop to demand some wine and a kebab. In mistaking the outgoing message to be the 'real' me, she was furious that I was ignoring her. This, of course, gave me a great idea for future phone calls from her.

Surprisingly, she could be quite nice to me

... sometimes, occasionally offering to make a cup of coffee for example. Regrettably, she made the worst coffee ever, but I'd reply with a polite *'Later'* or *'thanks but not yet'*. These conversations could be repeated several times within a few minutes, she having forgotten that she'd already asked me. Often, the coffee would appear nonetheless with her snapping that I *'obviously did want it'* having *'made it myself and leaving it on the kitchen worktop'*. I tried to tell her that I hadn't and that she'd done it. This usually resulted in the coffee being flung at me because I was playing mind games again.

Cats ... awful creatures, sly, disloyal, smelly, claws, lots of hair and piss around the house to leave their 'mark'. Janet had one but I think it was her 'familiar' and shared all her charms. I believe she'd put the idea into Judith and Jack's heads before she got back on her broomstick and flew home one evening. They wanted one too and harped on continuously and eventually wore me down. However, I made a deal with Judith being that it would stay in the conservatory, that she'd look after it AND she stopped drinking. She agreed too willingly of course. The following day, not one but <u>two</u> kittens appeared at our house. As they grew, they became yet two more of my tormentors, dragging in all manner of wildlife, dead or alive.

Judith was desperate to carve out a notch in life for herself. In her twisted reality, this involved showering gifts on a whole range of people. Around this time, it was becoming a 'thing' for parents to buy gifts for teachers at the end of the academic year. Judith had to go large though, doing it at the end of every term – and not just for the class teacher but also the headmaster, the classroom assistants and even the school secretary. She would tell me that all the teachers and the other parents were going to the pub to 'celebrate'. So it was that school holidays got off to a costly and boozy start.

As I researched into coercive controlling behaviour in the years that followed, I was constantly amazed and mystified how even the most 'challenged' of controllers could continue to manipulate and manage those around them. One morning, just before the summer holidays, I was on the point of leaving for work at 8 am. She followed me, ranting that I hadn't said goodbye to her. As far as I was concerned, this wasn't surprising since we had spoken for about 3 days. Then she asked how I expected Jack to get to school. I'd naturally assumed that Dick would be taking him as usual but, on this occasion, he and Janet would be arriving late. So, I went back into the house, plonked Jack in the bath, dried and dressed him and made him some breakfast, which he wouldn't eat. All the while she was nagging me to go and get her some drink, which I did, only to keep her mouth shut. As I got back, I saw one of the other mothers at our house, opening her car door for Jack to get in. Judith had pre-planned it and had done all of this to stall me until the off-licence had opened.

I was becoming very concerned about her obscene language and behaviour with Jack. I'd asked my niece to join us that year at the Sunderland Airshow. While Jack and I reserved a patch of grass outside, Judith took my niece into the nearby hotel to get some 'refreshments'. She told my niece that she'd asked Jack what he wanted to do during the holidays. The reply, according to Judith was, *"To play with your fucking fairy and beep your horns!"*. She conveyed this with great glee but made my niece promise not to tell me. The fact that I'm repeating this here shows where my niece's loyalty lay and reveals the horror she felt!

While tidying the house one evening, after Judith and Jack had gone to bed, I came across a childlike drawing of a naked woman, complete with enormous breasts. The word 'MAM' was scrawled across it, with an arrow pointing to what appeared to be Kielder Forest in the pubic area. I tackled her about if the following day and she told me he'd drawn it the previous morning. I thought it might be time to sit down with him and ask him why he'd done it before telling him not to do it again. As I sat with him, he noticed the paper and asked what it was before I could say anything. I showed him and with wide eyes and a shocked expression he asked, *"Who did that?!"*. I took a closer look at the handwriting and realized that I'd been had! He disappeared into the kitchen and returned with another piece of paper. This was scrunched up and he offered to me as if to prove a point. He was clearly embarrassed about it as I read a string of obscenities on the back. It was all in her handwriting but, as she entered the room at that point, rather than risk her rage, he 'admitted' that he'd done this too!

Judith continued to sleep with Jack up to and beyond our breakup. She would be naked or wearing only panties. Jack was 8 and the sight of him asleep with one leg on her huge belly and a hand on one of her nipples filled me with disgust. By now, I was getting concerned over his sleeping arrangements at his grandparents, wondering if this behaviour was 'normal' in that family. She also often shared a bath with him and teased him about intimate parts of his body. She would lie there, cuddling him, making comments about the size of his penis, referring to it as a 'parrot's beak'. When I asked why he got in with her he said that she just got in with him and lay on top of him. She even took him into the toilet with her and I dreaded his friends ever finding out. Jack was also told that eating tomatoes was good for 'his privates'.

Whether they be friends or strangers, she became obsessed with the accidents or tragedies suffered by other people. She HAD to become part of the story. I'd known Dave for over 30 years and it was a ritual of ours to spend every other Friday evening together in the Blue Bell Inn in Stanley. She resented our friendship and made serious attempts to drive us apart, even claiming that he'd made several passes at her. Now, Dave was a man for the ladies but he wasn't desperate enough or I'd say brave enough, to have a go at her. She definitely wasn't his type and the whole thing was laughable. One evening, I was reading the obituaries in the local paper and came across the name of the landlord of the Blue Bell. Dave and I knew him well and I called him to tell him of the passing of our favourite host. Two days later, Judith presented me with the news that 'Brian' wasn't dead – it was his father! She didn't know Brian and had never been to the Blue Bell. That didn't stop her obsessively spending time and effort, investigating. Having drawn a blank, she'd resorted to calling the pub to ask, *"Is Brian the landlord dead?"*. Brian having answered the phone, was rather taken aback. He later asked me whether he should be worried! Judith was extremely pissed off when I announced that I'd known about Brian's dad since my conversation with Dave.

There was no love lost between Judith and my niece but, having been kicked by a horse, Katherine had been hospitalised. I mentioned to Judith because I was going in to see her but didn't tell her what had happened. Why should I? She had no interest in the kid anyway. That didn't stop her methodically calling all the local hospitals to trace her to find out more information. After all, she was family.

Soon after this, I'd returned from work with a sore eye, which grew more painful as the evening wore on. I'd accidentally rubbed some chemical into it and knew I needed treatment. I told Judith what had happened although she was skeptical. Managing to drive to the nearest NHS drop-in centre, I was given an hour-long irrigation of the eye. It then had to be checked for damage. During the course of the treatment, we were interrupted by the medical receptionist who told us that a 'lady' claiming to be my wife had been repeatedly calling to ask whether I really was there. The receptionist had refused to confirm this because she found the caller 'suspicious'. By the time I got home, Jack was awake and up, in floods of tears, because *"Dad had gone off to see his girlfriend!"*

One of the other mothers had sadly been diagnosed with a brain tumour. Judith wanted me to take her to the woman's house but I refused. I wasn't going to 'cold call' on a terminally ill person, especially with a pissed wife in tow. She became aggressive and agitated, Jack ran out of the house into the back garden and I followed, trying to settle him. However, she followed, shouting and swearing. This had now attracted the attention of the neighbours. Jack ran into the house and she rushed after him. He said something, I'm not sure what, but I caught her telling him that she *"Didn't like (him) either!"*

Even after we'd split, she was still hounding me. One Friday, I told her that I wouldn't be able to see Jack the following day because I was in hospital. She demanded to know why and I told her I had a suspected Deep Vein Thrombosis, my leg having swelled up and being very painful. When I was released on the Sunday, I was greeted by a torrent of texts accusing me of being a liar. She claimed that she'd called 'all the local hospitals' and there was no record of me being at any of them! Jack had been told that it was simply an excuse because I hadn't wanted to see him!

The year before we split, she developed a long-lasting craving for cheese savoury sandwiches. She wanted me to get them for her before I took Jack to school at 830am. These, of course, were the days long before Greggs opened before 900am! I told her that I'd also fetch her some rocking horse shit as that would be more plentiful at that time of the morning. One evening, I was on my way home at 8pm having been estimating all afternoon on Teesside. She'd been repeatedly calling me throughout the day to get her a cheese savoury sandwich and by this time, I was getting pissed off, knowing full well that I wouldn't be able to get one. It now became a matter of life or death. Oh .. and by the way .. *'two bottles of wine'*. I decided to go to ASDA, grabbed a basket and flew around grabbing cheese, coleslaw and bread buns ... and, of course, wine! I rushed home, burst through the door and screamed *"MAKE YOUR OWN FUCKING CHEESE SAVOURY SANWICHES!"*. I glared in her direction but was disappointed to see that she was now fast asleep in the armchair. I was never too keen on cheese savoury sandwiches.

THE BATTLE FOR INDEPENDENCE

Our relationship had developed out of an adulterous affair and despite, or possibly because of, this, Judith didn't trust me and was forever suspecting me of 'wandering'. She did all she could to 'prevent' me, *"Nobody is going to want an ugly fat pig"* was the oft repeated phrase. The fact was that I had no thoughts of it but that wasn't what she believed. Her solution was to try to control me at every moment of the day.

I was a member of a national damage management group and, one September, was invited to attend a masterclass in Bristol. It was a one-day event and was going to be great opportunity to promote the business and do some networking. Because of the distance, I decided to drive down the previous day and drive back the day following the class. This meant two night's stay at a Travel Lodge. Hypocritically, despite the Marriott being a favoured choice of accommodation for her, she was livid at the prospect of me staying away in a hotel. She refused to believe that the trip was genuine and, when I showed her the documents, she then decided that she'd 'come along'. I told her that she was paranoid and not thinking. Jack would still be at home. Besides, she had no invitation and had nothing to contribute. She would be an embarrassment but, when I told her there would be no mini bars at a Travel Lodge, she started to have second thoughts. However, over the coming days, she continued to accuse me of cheating, in front of Jack, and said she'd make my life 'fucking hell'. At this point Janet joined in and I was getting it all in stereo. Janet said she and Dick would be looking after Jack but this would be totally impractical too since it would involve a 30-mile round trip each day. I then pulled a master stroke by insisting that, if Judith was to come with me, then Jack must stay with MY parents. They decided to back down but only if I agreed to travel by air and therefore be there and back the same day.

Judith checked up on me at every opportunity. She would trawl through the messages and texts on my cell phone, open and read my mail and even check that I was wearing 'appropriate' clothing for the workshop. One day, on getting ready in the morning, I couldn't find any clean underwear. I realised that the washing hadn't been done. Strangely, there were none in the washing basket either, despite it being full although the greater part inside was made up of empty bottles. I decided to 'go commando' because I was running late and couldn't afford to lose any more time.

As I was leaving, she demanded that I drop my trousers and prove that I was wearing underpants! I wasn't about to show her and Janet my bare arse at that time in the morning and continued on my way with her ranting that I was wearing none because I was on my way to see another woman.

As Christmas approached, life became more risky. It was my habit to buy small gifts for my business customers. On the evening of one 16th December, I went into the study and closed the door behind me. Judith and Jack were in bed, upstairs. I set about wrapping the presents plus another two for Judith. I was sitting on the floor, close the door with my back to it. Suddenly the door burst inwards with considerable force. I went flying along with many of the gifts, which I was wrapping and placing in small gold gift boxes. She screamed at me for buying presents for my 'girlfriends' and, when I told her what I was doing, I was demoted from a cheater to a 'puff, sending gay boxes'. She proceeded to attack them, tearing them apart and throwing them around the room. Wild and out of control, she laid into me. I didn't retaliate but instead calmly and silently started to put everything back together under her watchful, silent glare.

The following morning brought some

extraordinary 'admissions'. She said that she was drinking for a couple of reasons. The first was that she'd received a phone call from a woman who told her that I'd slept with her while at a seminar in Glasgow. I *had* been to such a meeting several months earlier and had travelled there and back the same day, by train. Judith said she had dates and details and 'knew everything'. It was pure fantasy, of course but her bare faced nerve just showed how good she was at manipulation. She never did give me the second reason.

I once made the mistake of buying myself some deodorant and putting it in my briefcase until I got home. I'd forgotten about it until she stormed into the living room and clobbered me about the head, twice. She'd been into the case and found the deodorant, which was obviously so that I could smell nice for my 'whore' I told her not to treat me that way and she told me to 'FUCK OFF'. I reminded her that it was me who worked all day, 6 days a week and I wouldn't be told how I spent my money. Besides, the £4 it cost was a fraction of what she was spending every day on booze. However, she lived in the belief that what was hers was hers and what was mine was also hers.

Her abuse of our joint account ran us short for trivial things .. like the mortgage. It also

meant that I was struggling for find cash for other things such as Christmas. Before I took the drastic action of setting up a new account in my name, I had decided to put some money regularly into a small personal account I'd had for many years. I'd had it re-registered to our address because it had been recorded at my parents' since I was a child. I wrote to the bank and asked them to re-register it to my parents' so that Judith, while opening my mail, wouldn't see any statements and begin hounding me for more money. This was all to be put aside for Jack. This bit me on the backside when the bank wrote to me to confirm the instruction. This letter, of course, went to my current address. When Judith opened it, the shit really hit the fan. I was trying to build a route out of the marriage and move back in with my parents. Telling her that I'd done it to stop her pissing Jack's Christmas down the toilet, really didn't help. After that, any financial transaction I made was yet another piece of treachery in her mind. Even a scam invoice and request for payment from an address in Czechoslovakia was proof that I was now operating overseas bank accounts.

Ironically, by this time, I'd paid off a huge amount of her debt … £12,000 off her own credit cards and £2,000 off a joint account she had with Janet. They couldn't pay them and debt collectors were gathering. She still had another credit card with a £15,000 balance on it, however. My own credit card was also standing at £15,000 although this had been accumulated mainly to keep Judith in the manner to which she'd become accustomed. I shopped around and found some 18-month interest free balance transfer deals and arranged for the balances to be moved. She agreed to it on one of the rare occasions she was relatively coherent. Then she promptly forgot and, for the next few years, she randomly accused me of conning her, forging her signature and syphoning money off her.

She contributed nothing to the business when she was employed there. Her antics, absences and neglect had brought us to the eve of prosecution by the Inland Revenue because she'd continually failed to report the payroll figures and complete the year end. This was part of the reason why I had to take her out of the business and she said she'd log a claim for benefits. True to form, though, she was too idle to do even that.

VIOLENT TIMES

I'm not about to dispute that domestic violence is more commonly committed by men. That much is self-evident, dreadful and inexcusable. I do find myself wondering about the statistics, though. It's said that 1 in 7 of all incidents of domestic violence is committed AGAINST men. If most who are targets act like me and keep it hidden, it's going to be very much understated and under recorded. Why should it be kept hidden? Because I'm a man and ashamed to admit that I've been physically assaulted by a woman, ashamed to admit that I didn't protect myself, ashamed to admit that I didn't take action to fight back, ashamed to admit that I didn't report it. Why didn't I do these things? Simple – I was protecting the family household for the sake of my child. Was I right? Probably not, but when you're gripped by a storm, all you can do is hold on and hope.

Even before we started our affair, Judith wasn't shy about giving me the odd 'bat'. At first, I was amused and saw it as physical 'teasing'. It seemed to be her way of making physical contact. As time went on, the bats became harder and were definite 'thumps' in front of others as she seemed to be trying to stamp her territory. She slapped me hard in the face while I was driving with her and 3 other colleagues in the car. Quite apart from being dangerous, she'd embarrassed me and I told her so, firmly. By that time, however, the damage had been done.

Over the years, I'd become accustomed to her punches and scratches and even became a bit blasé about them. It was only after Jack was older and became aware of what was going on that it became a real problem for me. The attacks got worse now and, yet I couldn't react out of fear of totally traumatising him.

When he was seven, I'd collected him from Dick and Janets' one Sunday morning after he'd spent the night there. I was taking him to his 'tag' rugby practise when, on the way there, he told me that he didn't want to go with Judith to the Marriott hotel that afternoon, to go 'swimming'. We talked about it and I suggested that I take him to a fun park instead, which he thought was a great idea. As we pulled into the rugby club, she called and, over the hands free, asked him if he still wanted to go swimming at the Marriott. He told her he didn't and wanted to go to the fun park instead. She became riled and started to pressure him. However, he stuck to his guns despite being told that he'd be bullied at the fun park. She slammed the phone down and, when we got back home, she was still raging. After a few drinks she started to calm down and even drifted off to sleep. We sneaked out and headed for the park. Within half an hour she was back on the phone, demanding that I go back with him. I refused saying that the day was his. We eventually got home at 6pm after also visiting my mam and dad. This lit the blue touch paper. I was depriving her of Jack and taking over her life. Her parents weren't being allowed to see Jack. She paced back and forth, frantically beating herself around her head before launching at me, winding me in the process. I was floored and Jack pleaded with her to stop, asking why she was hitting dad. She spent the rest of the night crying before admitting that she'd been wound up by Janet and Dick. They'd told her that they had no more money and wouldn't be able to come over more than once a week. At this news I could hardly contain my excitement but she was devastated and told me that if her parents couldn't see Jack, then neither could mine. She insisted that Jack would be devastated and that I had to give them money. I told her that Dick and Janet probably had more money than us but she refused to accept that. This was all about Janet trying to stop access to Jack by my parents, of course. My parents had 'lots of money' they said. She then threatened to start self-harming.

There were two main triggers for her violence. One being if Jack spent time with my parents and the other being when she was craving alcohol. She would relentlessly nag me for booze, no matter the time of day or what I was doing. There were threats that Jack wouldn't be allowed to do this or that. She pleaded and begged. If I didn't play ball, the violence began. Her weapon of choice was her long nails which she would use to shred my throat or arms. The wounds would often become infected and were visible, much to my embarrassment. She would hit me around the head and gouge my skin even as I sat with my arms around Jack, trying to comfort him. Once she got my briefcase and proceeded to tear up all the documents inside. Jack would often plead with her to stop, saying that he'd kill himself. She laughed.

One night, I decided I'd had enough and went upstairs to pack a suitcase with the intention of going to my parents' for the night. They both followed me with her laughing hysterically. Jack didn't want me to go and grabbed the suitcase. I realised that I couldn't do it as he was terribly upset and, of course, vulnerable. Besides, why should I leave? She was the problem, not me, it was MY house. I went back downstairs and sat with my head in my hands, with Jack cuddling me. She followed again, all the while laughing and demanding wine. She had the nerve to accuse me of upsetting Jack.

Because Jack was so upset, I gave in and went to get her the booze – but not before telling her what a lousy mother she was. She laughed again. When I got back and out of Jack's hearing, I told her to get a solicitor. She said she'd already seen one and she was going to get most of what we had, half the business and, of course, Jack. I returned to Jack who eventually fell asleep. As I carried him upstairs, I told him how much I loved him. Soon after, she appeared, stripped off and got into bed with him.

I thought that the violence was directed only at me. One January day, something happened to make me wonder. She'd been arguing with Jack because he said he wanted to go with me to the off-licence. She'd already attacked me and followed him into his bedroom. When I heard him crying, I jumped up and ran to him, finding him distressed with tears rolling down his cheeks. I asked him what was wrong and he told me that she'd bounced his head of the bed frame. She angrily denied it but he insisted that she'd done it. Then he reminded her that she'd hit his head with a chair the previous week. She denied that too, becoming hysterical and accusing him of being a 'nasty person'. He asked her to say sorry, but she wouldn't and still she refused to allow him to go with me. I snarled at her, telling her I'd get the wine but if I ever found out that she had hit him, it would be the end of the marriage and I'd have no problem reporting her to the police.

As far as I was aware at the time, that was the only episode of her aggression towards Jack. I was wrong. She would be aggressive with him behind my back if she thought he was spending too much time with me. She told him that he should be spending time with her instead but could never bother herself to entertain him. He'd try to avoid an argument by saying *"Whatever"*. Then there'd be a full-blown row, usually getting me involved. He'd run into the kitchen and sit on the floor with his hands over his ears. He later said to me that he wanted to run away but only wanted me to know because he didn't want to speak to her.

I took him to Toys R Us after work and shortly after the bed incident. He was hungry and hadn't been fed, so we called at the chip shop. I asked him if he was afraid of his mam. He told me he was and especially if he tried to talk to her about her drinking and she got angry. He also got frightened when he couldn't wake her. He told me that she 'hit him hard' and that he was also 'a bit worried about other things (but) 'couldn't explain'.

I became more and more aware of how much she deliberately intimidated him, especially to stop him telling me if she hadn't fed him or had been asleep when he was alone in the house with her. I'd taken him to a leisure pool one day and, on the way back, asked if he'd like a McDonalds. He said he probably shouldn't even though he was hungry. *"You know what mam's like"* he said, shrugging his shoulders, *"She'll go mad!"* In his mind he was convinced that, by me feeding him, she would say that I'd be trying to take him away from her. Once again told me that he was afraid of her although I told him he shouldn't be because she loved him very much. It was **me** she was angry at and none of this was his fault. With that he seemed to settle. I took him through the drive-thru and he belly laughed as I impersonated the staff.

He often wanted to sit with me while he was eating. That didn't suit her one bit and she became agitated, demanding to know why and accusing me of turning him against her. As he'd predicted she told him that 'his head had been turned' (this was a Janetism). She told me that he didn't really want to be with me, he was just trying to please me. She dragged him off to bed but he sneaked back after she fell asleep because he was afraid and didn't want to be alone with her. Besides, she also 'crushed' him.

A couple of days later, while I was washing the dishes, he came to me clutching his stomach. He told me that she'd punched him ... hard! She ran in behind him, ranting gibberish in an infantile way. *"He started it!"* she shouted and called him a *"Whingy Baba"*. She then went on to make the outrageous allegation, *"What about the time you broke my nose and I had to tell the doctor what you did!"*. This horrified him and was a terrible lie. Yes, she'd been to see the doctor having been suffering from nose bleeds. This was another indication of her alcoholism, along with the bruising. She'd tried to tell the doctor that he'd caused the bruising by hitting her in his sleep. She also claimed that he'd broken a bone in her foot. He was very disturbed and wanted me to know that none of this was true. I reassured him that I knew.

I began to look to past events with a different eye now. When he was six, she called me, panicking, while I was on my way to work because he'd hurt his arm. I found him in agony and rushed him to A&E. She'd refused to go with us, which I found strange at the time. I carried him from the car park to reception and we were seen immediately. He had a broken collar bone. I quizzed her when we got home and she told me that he'd fallen off the bed. To this day, I wonder.

TIGHTENING THE GRIP

Janet and Judith's attempts to control Jack's every waking moment accelerated as time went on, often masked as generosity but, in fact, being obsessive control.

From utter pettiness such as complaining to the headmaster that other kids were excluding him from their games to ridiculous overspending on him just before Christmas, it was a roller coaster of manipulation for him.

On every occasion they went out, they had to return with a 'present' for Jack and we're not talking about the odd packet of sweets or trinket. These were seriously large and expensive gifts bought on credit cards. When these were at their limit, while Judith was still involved in the business, the company cash card was used. His 8th birthday 'party' for him and three friends cost over £1,000. However, the alcohol element was nearly half of that because there were more adults than children. As the afternoon wore on, Judith and Janet demanded that I take the kids to a fun park in the evening, so the adults could continue celebrating. I refused and was accused of spoiling his birthday.

For Judith, and especially Janet, Jack was a 'possession'. They shifted their own insecurities and fears onto him and turned him into a very insecure child. This was especially true if he was ill and developed diarrhea or worse, vomiting. Judith couldn't handle any of that and would stand, screaming at him, and this was her idea of 'maternal instinct'. He developed a phobia of going to the toilet and many days would go by before he eventually moved his bowels, sometimes even a couple of weeks. This was clearly the result of stress but Judith was having none of it and was extremely intolerant. She would plonk him on the toilet and sit there shouting at him or threatening to take him to the doctor who'd *'stick his finger up (his) bum!'*. That terrified him but not as much as the threats to take him to hospital to be operated on. Of course, none of this worked and I'd often find him crying in the bathroom, sat on the loo with his trousers around his ankles. I discreetly bought him some palatable laxatives which helped him, until Judith found out and threw them out. There was no change over the next few weeks and he let slip to me that he'd been bleeding 'down below'. She was aware of it but had done nothing. I found blood in his underwear and managed to get an urgent doctor's appointment. He was scared and couldn't even produce a urine sample because 'it was burning'. Nevertheless, the doctor prescribed him with something to tackle the infection and advised me to continue to give him the mild laxatives. In the meanwhile, her hysteria did nothing to improve matters.

Jack always reached for me if he was poorly and she was happy for him to do that because she couldn't stand it. If I was at work, she'd have Dick and Janet take him to their house. However, he was learning and figured out that, by telling her he wasn't well, it was a sure-fire way of getting out of having to go to the Marriott hotel, or the pub, or the off licence .....

His stamina was low and he was prone to gasp for breath if he did anything strenuous. Judith and Janet had taken him to the doctor and told him that asthma ran in their side of the family. Jack was then given inhalers to use. It didn't seem like asthma to me and I wondered if it was stress related. In fact, 18 years later and thanks to a post COVID consultation, a hole in his heart was discovered which had been there since birth and missed.

Judith would make no effort to protect Jack from the effects of her addiction. In fact, she relished telling him in every detail, trying to make him worry for her. It worked especially as he saw her being carted off constantly by ambulances. Then, one day in late 2006, there was a change. She had another episode while he was home alone with her. At 7 years old, he called an ambulance for her, himself although he was afraid to tell me afterwards for fear of her temper. While he was distressed by this episode, he eventually came to be blasé to the point when any blue lights passed us, they were *'on their way to see mam'* accompanied by eye rolling.

The following month, Judith was hospitalised. She'd woken up feeling dreadful and trembling. Dick, who'd arrived a little later, called the ambulance as she requested, while I got Jack fed and ready for school. As we left, he said she was *'silly'* for calling 999 *'just because she was feeling sick'*. I returned having dropped him off, to find Judith and Janet in the ambulance being whisked off to hospital. I followed and later was told that she would be kept in for a week. In the afternoon, I went to Jack's school to tell the headmaster that she wouldn't be at work that week before speaking to Jack to tell him. He took it worse than I thought he would. I asked my parents to collect him after school and give him his tea. I picked him up after work with the intention of taking him in to see his mam. He refused to go, claiming he was sick and tired. I quietly insisted and we drove off with him sobbing uncontrollably and pleading with me to take him home. It was pitiful but, having pulled over to talk to him, I somehow persuaded Jack that it was the 'right' thing to do. We weren't there more than a few minutes, however, much to the anger and suspicion of Judith and Janet who within hours were furiously having a go at me for taking Jack ice skating, along with my niece. THEY had wanted to take him apparently. Katherine was a 'bad person' and I was reminded of this 'betrayal' for years to come.

Whenever Jack called me from home, I'd instantly known when something was wrong. He learned to stop telling me that he was frightened and alone or when his mother was crashed-out or ill. Instead, he'd tell me that HE was feeling poorly. He used the term 'drowsy' a lot. I'd then go home to check up on him, usually to find her asleep, very pissed or in the throes of the shakes. There were some subtle changes in his reactions to her 'episodes'. *"Oh no not again!"* as he ushered me into another room, leaving her to it.

He enjoyed visiting my parents but was always on edge and anxious to leave. He didn't want Judith or Janet to find out where he'd been, because of their hostile reaction. For example, together with my mam, he'd made a plaster of Paris Egyptian moulded figurine during one visit. He was so proud of it and asked whether he could take it home. His intention was to give it to Judith as a present or kind of peace offering. When we got home though, she rubbished and threw it to the floor, smashing it and his spirit together.

I saw her destroying a model he'd spent all afternoon making from a kit my parents had bought him. He cried for me and she turned on him demanding to know why he wanted his dad now when he hadn't wanted him for the past 7 years! She stormed off into another room with him begging her to come back. She wouldn't and he eventually cried himself to sleep in my arms, asking why mam was so angry at him?

Jack's relationship with his mam was very complex. He loved her but feared her, he hated her drinking but thought the way she played with him if and when she was sober, was wonderful, he looked forward to having friends over but dreaded them seeing her drunk .... On her 37th birthday, he wanted to buy her some flowers and a card. We were about to leave, when he suddenly raced back into the house and emerged with his money box. Inside was a single £1 coin. He asked whether that would be enough to buy her some vodka too! His love for her was so great that he'd give all he had to buy her the very evil that was making his young life so miserable.

Jack and I were very close. He needed me and turned to me whenever he was sad, ill or frightened. I loved him with every part of my being and yet, tragically, this sparked the very jealousy and obsession from his mother and grandparents which caused his fear. By staying, I opened him to all of this plus the arguments and violence. There was no peace and he was torn between us, loving us both but hating what we were doing. He couldn't bear the prospect of his mam and dad fighting over him.

He was too aware of adult problems and would often 'listen in' from around corners. When I challenged Judith about her not processing the Tax and National Insurance, resulting in action by the Inland Revenue, she told me that she didn't care and hoped I went to prison. He then popped up his head and protested, *"I CARE!"*. He was so worked up about it that he offered me his own savings. From that point on, I did my best not to discuss such things in front of him, even if it meant soaking up everything Judith and her parents threw at me, like a sponge.

At the height of Judith's drinking, Jack's diet during holidays was woeful if I, or even his grandparents, weren't around. Breakfast would typically be a cereal bar, lunches would be McDonald's chicken nuggets and fries and sometimes, he went without food until I got back from work and became aware of what had been going on. Judith's shopping baskets would be full but more often than not with booze, topped up with sweets and cat food. Human food was rare and the cats ate better than Jack. There were even days when she used his dinner money to buy alcohol.

Despite all, Jack was a very bright lad and, at least initially, his academic achievements were very good. He was clever and imaginative. This showed his strength of character but, on the odd occasion he needed help and I stepped-in, there was hell to pay. Eventually, he stopped asking me because of all the aggravation. He was sensitive and, understandably, hated fighting. Occasionally, he'd have run-ins with other kids but Judith wouldn't support him, calling him a 'softee' or she'd scream at him for not defending himself. She even enrolled him in kick-boxing classes to 'toughen him up'. He hated these but never more so than when she joined-in and was pulled up by the tutor for her drunken antics. Perversely, on other occasions, Judith and Janet would beat a path to the headmaster's door for the most trivial of reasons when he had an argument with another kid.

His attendance at school began to slide as

Judith's condition deteriorated. Before and after we split, he would often complain of feeling ill or sick. After we split, she would keep him off at the drop of a hat. There was a pattern and this usually happened on a Monday, after their heavy weekends and on a Friday, as he dreaded the weekend to come.

Judith monopolised all his school activities. She and Janet would deliberately keep from me, the dates of his Christmas services or tell me only after they'd taken place. When he was seven, I enrolled him in a local all-day summer school. He enjoyed that until one day when his mother and grandparents turned up to take him out of it. This was because Dick and Janet 'needed' to see him at home. When I found out, I was furious and told Judith that I'd be taking him back the following day. However, they were determined to stop him going and I lost my temper at their selfishness, calling them 'useless pieces of shit!' So, there was another row resulting in her telling me that she was going to leave me and take Jack with her. He was crying and screamed at her, telling her that he wouldn't go with her. She demanded to know why he wanted to be with me but wouldn't go near her. She 'reminded' him that they'd all agreed to it. I pleaded with her to stop talking like that, but it fell on deaf ears. He ran out of the house and, finding him sitting on the front steps, I apologised to him for upsetting him, but he told me that it wasn't my fault. Truthfully, it *was* my fault, because I'd reacted to her when I'd previously decided not to let her provoke me into arguing in front of him. He soon asked me to take him to bed, which I did and told him stories until her constant yelling fell silent. After a while, and a bottle, she crawled upstairs and slipped into bed with him.

Jack hated the way she slagged me off in front of neighbours, his friends, parents of his friends and her school colleagues. He was ashamed and frustrated when his friends turned around and told him how much they 'hated' me. Fortunately, her school career was about to be cut short when she was told not to return. Jack once asked if he'd been born before we were married. I told him he was, to which he replied, *"You shouldn't have got married – then there wouldn't have been any arguments"*. Out of the mouths of babes, as they say …

Before and after we split, I made determined efforts to do things with Jack at weekends and during holidays …. have 'adventures'. It might be local, the seaside or country, or further afield. I tried to add in educational inspiration too. Castles, museums, fun parks, the beach, the countryside, waterfalls, Lake District, Centre Parcs, Whitby, steam railways ….. a real variety. This greatly frustrated Judith and her parents whose journey plans rarely went further than a pub. Consequently, there were more rows and I was accused of 'turning his head' again. Eventually, he became hesitant to go with me, saying he felt ill but I knew it was because of all the hounding and questioning he got when he returned. On the few occasions we went out as a family, Judith embarrassed him. She would get tanked up before we went to the movies, talk all the way through the film, much to everyone else's annoyance and leave halfway through to go to the bar. Once the movie had ended, it was almost impossible to get her to leave and the looks from other movie goers made us want to crawl under a rock.

On some occasions when another parent invited Jack over, she would tag along, drunk and again embarrassing him. Stories also began to circulate about me beating Judith. These rumours had come from Judith. She raged at Jack one day for 'saying things' to his friends. Apparently, he'd told them that his mam drank 'all the time'. She warned him to watch what he was saying because he'd be 'taken away'. As the stories spread, Jack became more and more isolated.

If I was at work and he was in the house alone with her while she drank and got blitzed, he'd go into the kitchen and form a kind of protective 'tent' between two cabinet doors. He'd sit inside so he felt safe and call me, pleading that I came home. This shocked even her and she'd usually then promise to stop drinking. I was past caring by now. She disgusted me. For his part, Jack wished there was a 'pill' to make her stop drinking. *"It's not your fault dad, it's the wine!"*

THE HOLIDAYS THAT NEVER WERE

What should have been happy, family memories were instead, times of the greatest stress. My journal entries continue to shock and shame me:

24th December 2006

Arranged to go to see Dorothy (my former deputy head teacher, economics teacher and friend) as I do every Xmas. Despite my best efforts, Judith came along. She invited S to Xmas dinner! She's incapable of cooking even for herself!

Started cleaning the house this afternoon. Spent 4 hours on the oven – disgusting! Still at it at 8 pm. She demanded that I stop because I was embarrassing her! She'd had 3 bottles of wine. None left so she drank her grandad's sherry too!

10pm – just finished. The house was a shit hole. Had to nip out to the workshop to get a part for the radiator cabinet. Got back to find that she's trashed the living room and smashed up the CD player! She's crying, depressed, miserable, aggressive and argumentative. HAPPY XMAS!

Xmas Day 2006

She woke us at 2 am.

Among other things, got her a CD of Westlife. She

tried to play it forgetting that she'd smashed the machine up last night. However, I'd bought her a portable player too, but she demanded that I bin both presents! Jack said it would be a waste and she shouldn't throw presents away. She went mental. I've ruined her Xmas. Bad Bad Bad!

Took Jack to mam and dad's at 10am. Her mob arrived at 12. She's had 2 bottles and can't feel her legs or face. She got in the bath with Jack again – and she's farting bubbles. He's not happy!

Put the beef in the oven. She's now asked me three times if I've done it.

Her family left at 3 pm. Spent the rest of the afternoon playing with Jack. He said it's the best Xmas ever cos he got everything he wanted and I'd spent the day with him too! Poor kid.

Katherine called (my niece). Someone phoned mam and dad's house asking for me. No idea who it was so I wrote the number down. I called it but the young guy at the other end said he wasn't aware of the call. Shrugged it off as a misdial. Later heard Judith arguing with someone. She'd called the number and was accusing someone at the other end of having an affair with me!

Boxing Day 2006

Lost track of what she's drank today. A 3 litre box and 2 bottles of wine have gone though. At 3pm she was snoring her head off. Hasn't bothered with Jack at all so far.

7 pm. Jack and I watching Pirates of the Caribbean. She demanded he go to bed with her. He refused. Accused me of taking him away from her.

She went into the kitchen. We heard a crash. She'd dropped a bottle of wine on the floor. Cleaned it up and she started crying and apologising. This is getting beyond a joke. She's pushing everyone away by her moods and rage. She hadn't taken her meds. Had to go and get her another bottle.

27ᵗʰ December 2006

12 midnight. Miracle upon miracle! She hasn't climbed into bed with him. I'm going to have to sleep in the same bed as her now, though. Oh, lucky me! At least Jack will be OK though.

4 am. Jack came up thinking that he heard her shouting for him and threatening him to come to bed. Must have been a nightmare!

0830 am. She thinks she has a melanoma. Docs at 0950. Blood tests taken. Had to go back again because she'd forgotten to get her repeat meds.

Went shopping with Jack for his bedroom wallpaper. She called and said she was going back to bed. Took our own lunches back to find she'd been grilling salmon. The place stank and was trashed again. She got up and went mental because we didn't bring food in for her. She wanted a sandwich like mine. I gave mine to her. She refused, wanted to go to the pub. We didn't – so we took her and said we'd wait outside for her. She went ballistic and told us to take her fucking home!

3 pm. Ended up at the Highwayman anyway! Bought her lunch but she wouldn't eat it because my face 'was tripping me'. 2 more bottles on way back home. She went to bed and got up again at 7 pm.

2ⁿᵈ January 2007

She was in a bad way this morning. Craving, shaking and crazy. Went to Asda at 8 am but they didn't open until 830. Got 2 bottles.

This evening had to get more booze. She tried to get into bed with Jack. He told her to get lost. She waited til he drifted off and got in with him.

2ᴺᴰ AUGUST 2007

We're off to Butlins Minehead!

Dick and Janet staying at ours to look after the cats.

Got home at 230pm today. The 3 of them are pissed already. J said they'd been to the COOP to get booze but didn't want me to say anything – too much trouble!

Drove to Nottingham and stayed at a Travel Inn to break the journey. She was out of her skull and slept all the way. At dinner she had another 2 large glasses and bought an additional bottle. She hadn't taken her meds so I insisted at 9 pm. Bit of a panic – couldn't find them! She got pissed while Jack and I played.

3rd August 2007

Jack and I had breakfast while she finished off her dregs from last night. Hit the road but had to pull off half an hour later so she could buy some wine. Bought 3 small bottles.

Arrived at Butlins at 2pm. She went straight to the bar – double vodka and coke. Bought another bottle of wine and sank it in the room. Went to Pizza Hut for tea – more wine and then bought another bottle. Jack wanted to go 'gold panning' but she complained about her legs. Told her she was ruining Jack's holiday. Said I was using him against her.

4th August 2007

She disappeared with my wallet at 8am and took Jack to the supermarket. She got a bottle of vodka and a bottle of coke before leaving Jack and going to the toilet to empty most of the coke and topping it up with vodka. When she got back, I counted that we had £90 left out of £280 two days ago.

Went for a short walk. Jack was playing in the fort. Told her I can't take this anymore and our marriage was dead. She broke down and I felt sorry for her. I went back to the room for a jumper for Jack. Came back to find that she'd just spent another £16 on booze and was playing the gaming machines.

Lunch – she ate part of a chicken burger and then bought another bottle of wine. Jack and I went swimming. Got back to find her crashed out.

Tea – she had no food, only a large wine. Afterwards, took Jack to mini golf and gold panning. She went to the pavilion and had a large vodka. Had to get another £200 out. She spent another £35 on booze and gaming machines.

Taking Jack to Wookey Hole tomorrow. She doesn't want to go. Probably for the best because of the state of her legs.

5ᵗʰ August 2007

Jack and I set off at 815 am and got back 5 hours later. We had a great time! I'd left Judith £20 this morning – none left now. An empty ½ bottle of vodka on the drawers. Said she'd also been to bingo.

At lunch she again ate nothing. Jack had burger and chips and she had a large vodka and coke. Jack wanted to go swimming, but she wouldn't go. She bought another ½ bottle of vodka and a blue WKD.

Headed for the room but she had to stop several times. Eventually got back. I cleaned up and then took Jack swimming, to golf and back to the fort. Got back, planning to go for tea. Judith on phone to her mother. I'm wondering what Jack's going to do for entertainment for the rest of the holidays when we get back and I have to go back to work?

Teatime – she wouldn't come out of the room. She stayed drinking while Jack and I ate. She's had nothing today so took her back a hotdog. Jack and I went to see the beach fireworks. Got back at 10pm – she hadn't eaten the hotdog. Very little booze left and she was pissed. She vomited frequently through the night, getting into bed with Jack after each episode. He pleaded with her to get out.

6ᵗʰ August 2007

We're leaving for Longleat today!

She finished the dregs before we went for breakfast. Jack and I ate while she went to the supermarket. She headed for the toilets to mix the booze with the pop and then stopped off at the gaming machines (what she means by 'bingo'). She wanted to stay with Jack at the fort while I went back to pack, wash the dishes and tidy up.

We left for Longleat Safari Park. She had at least ½ bottle. No matter, Jack had a great time and really enjoyed it. Afterwards, we headed for Alton Towers.

Got to the Splash Landings Hotel at Alton Towers and I signed them in before emptying the car, taking the luggage to the room and parking up. She decided that she'd get a large bottle of cider.

At dinner, she decided to tell Jack about my ex wife, Wendy!!!! He was shocked and confused as he knew nothing of her. For the fixed dinner price of £25 each, she then had part of a bowl of soup and a large glass of wine. Afterwards, she went to the bar and bought a bottle of house wine for £15.

7th August 2007

She woke screaming. She'd only had half her meds yesterday. She needed alcohol badly, but none was available on site at that time of day. The din was awful and she was disturbing the other guests around us. Despite being hungry, Jack and I delayed breakfast, left the site to find her some vodka. Bought 1½ bottles from the nearest town. Got back, gave her ½ bottle and took Jack for breakfast. Got back to the room after eating to find she'd polished-off the bottle!

We headed for the fun park where she drank vodka mixed with orange pop. At lunch, she had a large glass of wine. She wanted nothing but soup. I managed to negotiate a child's dinner price for her. Jack wanted to go swimming at the hotel but was starting to shun her. She was screaming at me, accusing me of turning him against her. When we got back to the room, I let her have it and told her she was ruining his happiness!

We left her in the room with a bottle of wine and another ½ bottle of vodka (siphoned from the bottle in the car) . We went to the theme pool and had a brilliant time! When we got back, we dressed for dinner. She said she wanted to go too. We went to the restaurant but there was a long queue and she could hardly stand. We were given a buzzer which reserved our position and went back to the room to await the call. She had soup again and went back to the room alone. Jack and I rushed to finish our meals and get back in case she locked us out and fell asleep. I packed the suitcases for the journey home tomorrow and took the non-essentials to the car. Got back at 940pm and she started screaming at me demanding to know where I'd been. As a precaution for the morning, I prepared a bottle for her to wake up to. During the night, she was up and down from Jack's bed, shouting that she felt ill.

8th August 2007

Last day at Alton Towers

She drank the bottle I'd prepared and I had to get the rest from the car before breakfast. She decided she couldn't drink it neat so I had to go out and buy some mixers. Took Jack to breakfast at 915.Got back to the room to find there was a small amount of vodka left. Told her to mix it up for the amusement park but she didn't want it. Turns out that it was only water as she'd drank the bottle and put some water in to hide that fact!

We packed the rest of the luggage, checked out and headed for the car to leave the bags before we went into the park. She said she couldn't face it so I said we'd have to go home. She insisted we leave her in the car and went to the park on our own. We weren't happy about it but left for the monorail. On the way there we chatted. He asked whether I'd left Wendy to be with his mam!! Soon we both agreed that we felt bad about leaving her so we'd go back and head for home. He was heartbroken but felt it was the right thing to do. At the car, she was out of it! We set off and she suddenly woke with a start asking where we were going. Then she became terrified of what her mother would think and insisted we turn round and go back to the park. He said we would, provided she went with us. She agreed.

At the park, she could hardly walk. I said I'd take Jack and a few rides then go back for her. As we left, she shouted us back because she didn't want to be alone. I managed to find her a deckchair by the boating lake while we went off and she seemed satisfied and soon zonked. After 3 rides, he was becoming uneasy at leaving her. We picked up a couple of holographic key rings of us together on the water rapids, which he treasured. When we got back she was fizzing with rage because we'd 'left her too long'. We returned to the car, and left for home via an off licence.

On the way back, had to stop several more times for

booze. Got home at 7pm after calling at the COOP where she bought 2 bottles of wine and some soup.

At home, I unpacked the car. Then I took ill .. faint and shaky. Had to eat some sugar to pull myself together. Then she spotted the key rings and went berserk. Accused me of 'editing her out of the holiday'! She was terrified that Janet would see them. Jack got upset and asked me to throw them away. Then she bullied him to go up to bed with her and he went, whimpering as they climbed the stairs.

9th August 2007

Later today I asked Jack if he'd enjoyed his holiday. He said he had but it would have "been better if mam hadn't been there". He asked me if I'd enjoyed it and I told him I had, because I was with him.

WEAVING THE WEB

I decided to write this account of my experiences two years after my split from Judith. I did it because I needed to tell someone – if only myself! And so, it was a great part of the healing process. I also hoped that, one day, it could be used to share with other men in my situation because of the lack of help and support that was available to me – and the outright hostility from the organisations which were supposed to support families in crisis. At first, there was anger and resentment, then deep depression before acceptance and finally, forgiveness. I sit here writing it again now, 17 years later, reviewing my words, refining them and, hopefully, putting them into print so that others can share and take heart. In those years between then and now, I researched and learned a great deal about alcoholics, domestic violence and controllers.

An alcoholic doesn't always appear to be drunk and they can be experts in hiding their behaviour. Alcoholic controllers are successful and prolific liars until the burden of their lies eventually collapses around them. That's because the 'web' can no longer bear the weight due to them not being able to remember what they've said and to whom. They will inevitably blame someone else for their problems and ruthlessly manipulate and control those around them in order to keep a grip on their 'reality'.

Their selfishness knows no bounds, even if it's at the expense of their own children. I've seen Jack crying with tiredness and exhaustion and pleading to go home from the Marriott hotel bar, only to be constantly told *only five more minutes*. On the other hand, they can't bear anyone to be enjoying themselves if they're not involved and at the centre of things. Judith would set out to make Jack feel guilty if he went anywhere with me, telling him *Mam is going to be all alone*. This was a tactic that Janet mimicked. He would then sacrifice his own enjoyment to stay with her or would be unsettled unless she tagged along. This happened when I took Jack for a coach trip to Durham for his tag rugby team when he was seven. Parents were accompanying their children but Judith kicked up such as fuss that I had to leave Jack on the coach under the watchful eye of another parent and return home to get her.

Alcoholic controllers can be 'overly generous' and try to 'buy' friendship by lavishing entertainment or gifts on others. I was often made aware that Judith had given some of Jack's friends money out of his money box or given away his DVDs, toys or computer games, much to his distress.

They will also try to drive a wedge between their 'target' and his or her family because of their resentment at the bond between them. This can take many forms such as parental or grandparental alienation and physical violence or restraint. At first, it usually takes the form of the 'carrot' rather than the 'stick'. I've already described the lavish spending on 'presents' for Jack by Judith, Janet and Dick, especially when they were on booze trips. However, they would critcise and even destroy anything I or my mam and dad bought for him. This would go as far as reading my emails to find out whether I'd bought anything for him online. If I had from there or anywhere else, the result for Jack would be interrogation and fury. When he started playing tag rugby, I bought him a full strip and formal wear. We return home and went into his bedroom so he could get changed and try them on. She woke from her drunken stupor, barged into his bedroom and screamed at me for 'hiding' things from her. He should have tried them on in front of _**her**_, she 'hated (my) guts' and I was 'playing mind games'. She made it clear to Jack that he was NOT to wear the clothes because I'd bought them only to 'get' at her. She physically stripped them off him. In a seemingly miraculous change of personality, she then asked him if he wanted to watch 'Scary Movie' with her. He replied that he was *"More concerned about my family"*, meaning he wanted to stay with me. *"Can't you see what you're doing to him"* she raged before again accusing me of taking him away from her.

Taking Jack out for a day or even a half day was a traumatic experience. I've said that an alcoholic controller will try to restrict the movements of their targets. She would tell Jack that she was depressed and even 'dying' to stop him leaving the house. I found myself asking for her permission to take my own son out, to appease her. Ironically, she would then arrange for Dick and Janet, or his friends' parents to pick him up and beat me to it. Dick and Janet were more than happy to participate, such as the time when I'd arranged, with Judith's agreement' for my parents to take Jack to the Northumberland Country Fair. As my parents pulled up to collect him, Dick and Janet were bundling Jack in their car and sped off. Once, I took Jack to Vindolanda inside Hadrian's Wall. She wasn't happy but, fortunately she was pissed and dosing. We set off and had a great time on the way, talking and telling jokes. He belly laughed as we shot over the blind summits but then, the phone calls started. In the remaining minutes of the journey, she told him how much she missed him, told him she wasn't well and cried. We journeyed on in silence, walked to the fort, paid the entry fees and wandered in before he said *"Dad, I feel guilty"*. He said he was having fun and it wasn't right that his mam, wasn't. He asked if we could go back home and, so, we left.

There were occasions when I was welcome to take him out, but only on condition that I bought wine and vodka first. On one occasion, Jack had called me at work to ask what time I was coming home because he wanted to go swimming at the local baths. I told him I wouldn't be long and he was happy and put the phone down. Seconds later, Judith called spitting feathers that he'd called me without having the 'decency' to speak to her first. She wasn't going to allow it unless I took both of them to the Marriott and then a meal. I returned with a couple of bottles of wine and a bottle of strong cider, which worked a charm. Jack and I went swimming.

When it came to trying to isolate Jack and me from my family, Judith and Janet were ruthless. In November of 2006, my mother had fallen seriously ill, so I told Judith I was going to see her. Jack said he wanted to come with me and she launched into a tirade: *"You're 49 years old! Why do you need your mummy and daddy!? You're pathetic!"*. I made a mental note of the irony in this but didn't react because Jack was there with us. She made a threatening move towards me, but I didn't flinch. Instead, I knelt down to fasten my shoelaces when I felt a shearing pain in my scalp as she yanked my hair from behind me. I was in agony but Jack was still there, so I stood up, took hold of her arm and attempted to shove her along into the bedroom so I could give her a piece of my mind. She threw herself to the floor, screaming that I'd hit her and inviting Jack to come and see what dad had done! I left her alone and went into the kitchen where she followed me, punching my arms, back and chest with incredible strength. She demanded that I hit back, saying that's what she wanted. She was wild and out of control. I refused so she threatened me with her family. I replied that if they started on me, I'd call the police. She screamed at Jack, saying that I was going to have his grandma and granddad arrested! She eventually calmed down and went to bed with two bottles of wine. I went to the local NHS drop-in centre to get checked out.

The controlling behaviour had now extended to my own access to Jack, even to phone calls. Then the paranoia set in, 'Why was I calling him? What was I calling about? What was I calling him about? Something was going on, what was it? It was all very odd because I hadn't called him before 'this had to stop because it was upsetting Jack' .... She'd now trained him to repeat every word I said aloud whenever I called him. I'd just bought him a mobile phone which she took off him and then Dick and Janet bought him 'a more expensive and better one!'.

She began to control what I could and couldn't say to him. I couldn't tell him if I was going to the off licence for her, I wasn't to talk about her drinking in front of him, she tried to stop me going to the school parents' evenings and I wasn't to help him. In fact, Jack was struggling with maths at school. I'd discussed it with his teacher at one of the 'forbidden' parents' evenings and Jack had also told her. I wanted to support him so came home with a couple of course books and a DVD which she immediately destroyed. Jack and I were shocked and he told her that there was no need for it, that she was always 'winding me up asking for wine all the time'. I accused her of deliberately harming his education when he said *"Dad, you better watch out ... she's got a real temper!"*. Too late was the warning – her face was red and distorted with rage. She lunged at me and grabbed my throat, her long nails digging into my flesh and drawing blood. It damn well hurt so I went into the bathroom to inspect my wounds once I prised her hand off me. Then there was a violent 'BANG'. I rushed back out to find the dining room door torn off its hinges. The handle had been wacked with such force that there was a hole in the wall behind. Jack stool there open mouthed and wide-eyed as she denied having done it!

As Janet's presence grew ever more overbearing, both she and Judith saw my family as a threat. At first, Judith had got on very well with them and the relationship was even affectionate. This all changed as Janet made herself at home at our house. When Jack and I visited my parents, Judith would call to demand that we return 'immediately' because they 'needed' to see him. Mam and dad's access to Jack was becoming less and less frequent and on one occasion at a very young age he'd said to mam *"You're not my real grandma … I already have a grandma"*. The stress of being pig-in-the-middle was unbearable but by the time Jack started the Parochial school at the age of 6, I'd managed to put a system in place where mam and dad would take Jack to school after I dropped him at theirs and collect him at the end of the day. They'd feed him and entertain him until I finished work and picked him up. This way, Judith wouldn't be driving and Dick and Janet, who lived 15 miles away wouldn't be 'inconvenienced'. This worked well for a little while, until

Judith and her parents became deeply unhappy about the amount of time Jack was spending with my mam and dad. Shortly after his 7th birthday, then, Judith announced that she'd be 'taking back control of MY child'. Janet had successfully put so much pressure on Judith to do this that she'd increased her drinking with stress.

My 50th birthday happened in the week that Judith was drying out in hospital. Janet tried everything to get him to stay at their house, calling him the day before and telling him to go there. He asked me whether that would be OK. I said it wouldn't because we'd be spending my birthday (the next day) together. He told her what I said and she gave him the silent treatment *"Are you there, grandma?"* he repeated over and over. Eventually she answered, telling him that she was going to miss him 'terribly' and she was 'looking and touching' his photograph as they talked! He teared-up. However, despite all Janet's best wishes, we went to a pantomime that evening after enjoying a Burger King and this was one of the few times since he was very young that I saw him laughing uncontrollably to the point of splitting his sides! When I put him to bed that night, he said he was sorry I wouldn't get any presents tomorrow. I told him that being with him was going to be the best present of all. He'd had 'The best night ever!' and then quickly went to sleep.

We'd visited Judith every day while she was in hospital and did so the afternoon of my birthday. She asked what we'd be doing to celebrate and I told her that my parents would be treating us to a meal at TGI Fridays. She instantly became irate. UNDER NO CIRCUMSTANCES was that going to happen! She shouted at Jack and told him he was a *'changed boy'* after only 2 days. I was 'changing' him and 'taking him away' from her. She tried to get him to eat a full bag of sweets to spoil his appetite, but I stayed calm. That evening, I switched my mobile off while we were at the meal. Afterwards, when I switched it on, there was a torrent of voicemails accusing me of daring to 'disobey' her and lying to her. She was going to start drinking again the instant she got out of hospital. She was going to take Jack out every day 'to pubs!'. I erased all the messages but, later, she called Jack to tell him how angry she was that he'd been out with me and the rest of my family. She did that a further twice before he went to bed, crying and upset. Happy birthday to me.

On day five of Judith's confinement, I took Jack to rugby practice when he turned to me and said *"Dad, there's something different about you!"*. I asked him what he meant and said he couldn't quite decide before blurting out *"I know what it is! You're happy and laughing!"*. He said we were having a great *time 'just the two of us!"*. On day six, I took him and my niece to the ill-fated ice-skating session which ended with as much, if not more, fury.

Janet and Dick's role in causing strain between me and my family was pivotal. I was desperate to keep them in Jack's life – for both their sakes and his. I also wanted him to see how a normal family behaved. On one of the schooldays, I'd arranged for them to collect Jack, Judith suddenly announced that Dick would be doing it. I reminded her of the agreement and told her that I wasn't going to let me family be isolated from him. She started to cry but said that she'd tell her parents. Once she'd sheepishly told them, she put the phone down but there followed a steady stream of aggressive and hysterical calls from Janet. If Dick couldn't pick Jack up, then they were going to stay away from her! I told mam what had happened and she sympathized with Judith and suggested a compromise. She and dad would return Jack half an hour after he'd eaten. But that was still unacceptable to Janet and Dick. They 'needed' to see him …. They 'hadn't seen him for days!!' My family was 'trying to take over' and they were going to 'take back control'. Mam called Judith and gave her both barrels. She told her she was being childish and risked losing both me and Jack because of her behaviour. She told Judith that she'd *"Wanted to say these things"* to her for a while but had held off because of her 'illness'. Judith was both furious and devastated. My mam had been blunt to say the least and was now the devil incarnate. Judith immediately relayed all the gory details to Jack. When I got home, she was out of it, but he was awake and wanted to talk. We did and he said he would have been angry in my mam's place too. But he blamed the wine.

The three of them would seize on any opportunity to put down my family. When dad was helping me remodel our front garden, they called him 'Percy Thrower' while watching him, from the window toiling away. Dick would watch him while sitting on the front steps, drinking and smoking but occasionally giving his mobility car a polish. Never once did he offer to help. Judith would tell me that I hadn't been 'brought up properly'. She'd been raised to 'have fun'. None of her school colleagues 'liked' my parents. I used to pay for dad's car breakdown policy for his birthdays. When she found out, she said we were 'finished'. On the other hand, she was furious when I bought his birthday card 'To Dad from a

Loving Son'. She demanded to know why I hadn't got one from the 'Both of Us'. I lied and said I couldn't find one and, besides, I wasn't going to ask her to sign it because of the animosity. However, she tore open the envelope after I'd signed it and proceeded to overwrite it with her own scrawling signature. Then she called the card shop I'd been to asking if they had any 'From the Both of Us' cards. They confirmed they did and she demanded I go and get one so we could send it. Jack and I took the card up to dad and he was thrilled when his grandad gave him some toys to take home with him. When we got back, she told him they 'smelled' and threw them in the bin.

In late 2007, mam had become gravely ill with kidney failure and repeatedly hospitalised. Judith knew she was in hospital but I told her nothing given her attitude. Nevertheless, she made it her business to phone all the local hospitals attempting to find where she was. Having tracked her down to the Freeman Hospital, she demanded to know what was wrong with mam. She had a 'right to know' because she was her daughter-in-law. Mam asked that they told her nothing. Jack wanted to visit but Judith was absolutely against it. She told him that hospitals were full of diseases where people 'ripped their skin off' and killed people.

LEARNED BEHAVIOUR

Before Judith became a full-blown alcoholic, she was the type of person who made an effort to get along with everyone. She was attractive, outgoing and friendly. While she was inclined to be lazy, she was quick on the uptake, being very intelligent. It was her parents' damaging influence which turned her into the person she now was. By billeting themselves at our home, she could get no respite from the drinking and controlling.

Dick had lived off the state since he was 50 years old, having persuaded the DWP of his 'bad back'. He was highly skilled in maximizing his entitlements and his pride was his car provided by the Motability programme. He led a shallow life of little substance. His biggest fear in life was Janet who, to her credit, worked until she was in her mid-50s before she, too, was 'medically retired' on the grounds of 'depression'. Her arm trembled uncontrollably and my dad once asked he if she was OK, bringing on a tirade of abuse which shocked and appalled even Judith. She was on the same meds as Judith and it was her vicious temper and controlling personality which tainted the lives of those around her. Only Judith's brother had partially escaped. He had little to do with his parents and, when he had his own daughter, refused to let them have anything to do with her. Dick and Janet were deeply hurt and called him, with great irony, a 'nasty, selfish control freak'.

If Judith and Jack had gone to stay with her parents and I would call to see how they were, Janet would refuse to let me speak to them, telling me instead that Judith was 'having fun'. She would tell me with unbridled glee that they'd been drinking and Judith was laughing more than she'd ever seen. The inference wasn't subtle but I wouldn't argue because she was drunk herself. Once, when Judith called me from one of these 'respites' I suggested that she might want to consider going to her parents' more often if she enjoyed it so much because I couldn't cope with her and she'd be getting only one bottle of vodka from me. I was obviously on speaker and heard Janet's voice boom *"IT'S YOUR HOUSE TOO!"*. It became clear that the three of them had been discussing how get their hands on the house and whatever else they could leech away. Even if I organised mundane maintenance jobs, it was met with hostility, suspicion and blocking tactics on the grounds that I may be planning to sell the house and run off.

Apart from sitting on top of her, Judith was terrorized by the constant phone calls from

Janet. Having just got home, she'd call our house to speak to Jack. If he wasn't around she'd spit venom at Judith – *"It doesn't matter ... I hardly ever see the bairn anyway!"*. She even told her that Jack had said he'd rather live with her than stay at home with his mam who was a 'lousy mother'. Judith would often say that she wished Janet would stay away, only to backtrack moments later. She was addicted to Janet and Janet was addicted to Jack.

They saw it as their 'right' to be with Jack all of the time. Quite apart from the uproar which happened if my parents or even I spent with him, they went to ridiculous lengths to stop our contact. Rather than allow my mam and dad to look after him if they had appointments in the morning, they would drive the 15 miles to collect him and then return home with him before going to their engagements. They refused to leave the house until they'd seen him, meaning that, if he was with me or my parents, he'd have to come back home. If he didn't, he'd be met with a note telling him that they'd *'come all this way to see (him)'* but that he wasn't there, so they'd have to go home *'missing'* him and *'kiss (his) photo instead!'*. He'd feel so guilty that he'd often write on the back of the notes, telling them *'how sorry'* he was. Janet left such a note one evening when he was at kick boxing. I intercepted it and hid it from him. Then she called and spoke to Judith, demanding to speak to him and ask if he'd seen her letter. Of course, neither he nor Judith had, and Judith then started to frantically pull the house apart in sheer panic. Having not been able to find it, she called Janet back and offered to have him stay at her house for a few days instead as compensation! The cynical manipulation of the child was simply shocking.

It seems that, the following day, Janet had realised she'd gone over the top and brought a homemade corned beef pie as a sort of peace offering. Judith asked me to eat it, but it was vile. She pleaded that she wanted no trouble and Janet had said she'd go through the bins the next day to make sure I hadn't thrown it out. So, I took it to work and used the bin there.

Janet's expressions began to feature more and more *"It's a husband's place to provide for his wife!"* ...... *"There is no limit to what a wife should be entitled to"* ...... *"You're not indispensable!"*. The stopping of me or my family spending time with Jack because ever more blatant. If we'd organized something, on that morning they'd simply announce that they'd be taking him for the daftest reason, on one occasion, to go to *'Amy's birthday party'*. Amy was ninety years old!

One of the methods Janet used to bribe Jack

to spend more time with them would be used, eventually, to take him out of my life, permanently. That was to tell him that 'his friends' living around their house, had been knocking on their door, asking for him to go out and play. This was them gradually substituting kids from their village for his friends at home.

Both Dick and Janet were totally opposed to Judith receiving counselling for her addiction. They were hostile and blamed NECA, 24/7 and AA for the deterioration in her condition. They were desperate for their sordid family history, to remain secret. Judith had given me snippets about her childhood including Janet's temper, abandoning her at Butlins, whispers about affairs and her mother asking if her father had ever 'touched her'. It was clear that Janet was equally jealous of Judith's relationship with Dick, who she adored.

They were determined to outspend me when it came to Jack. I'd decorated his bedroom to replicate the inside of Dr Who's Tardis and laid a good quality blue wool twist carpet. I returned from work to find it torn up and replaced with their own choice – a cheap polyester version of exactly the same colour. If ever I bought him something, they would buy him the same and this eventually mushroomed into him receiving lavish, huge presents from them. He was given a large, sit-in battery operated jeep at 2 years old which he couldn't use because there was nowhere to play with it except on the busy road outside and he had a mobile phone at the age of four.

I found out that they were sleeping with him when he was at their house, I asked Judith to get them to stop. He had a separate bedroom and should be using it. She saw nothing wrong with it though. *"He's just a little bairn"* she said, but that was exactly my point (he was 6 years and older). I asked her what her parents were thinking, sleeping with a child but this only earned me another beating. While he was at their home, if I ever called to speak to him, I'd be accused of 'checking-up' on my own son.

Jack was often taken on holiday without my knowledge. I'd planned to take him and Judith to North Yorkshire, Scarborough, Robin Hoods Bay and Flamingo Land. Shortly before I'd made the arrangements, I found an itinerary for Flamingo Land for Thursday of that week on our mantlepiece. It turned out that Dick and Janet had used my credit card details to book it and a few more days away for the four of them. Jack told me this on our way to Prudhoe Pool that evening. He said he wished that I was going too. He asked me not to tell his mam that he'd told me because he'd been promised two Transformer toys if he kept the secret. He also warned me not to make a fuss because his grandma had told him that she and Judith had once made a voodoo doll of someone they hated. They stuck pins in it and the person had died!

I asked Judith how they'd be getting to Flamingo Land. She told me that she would be driving! I told her to get her father to drive because of her 'problem' and I didn't want harm to come to any of them, especially Jack. She stormed off and took Jack to bed. When the day came, it was obvious that Dick had no intention of driving. Rather than risk anything, I decided to take time off work and drive them all myself. Dick and Janet were 1½ hours late and didn't answer the 16 calls Judith made to find out where they were. I'd also arranged to collect all of them at the end of their short holiday but had to pay for an extra night's accommodation for them because I couldn't pick them up on the final day as a result of another commitment. Judith then demanded more money to see them over the extra day. I offered her £50 and she went ballistic. In the end, I had to give her another £100. I gave Jack £20 too, although she didn't like that. That evening, she called in tears, having been arguing with Janet about drink and 'other things'. Dick had tried to comfort her and said he would support her if she went back to see the doctor on their return. When I collected them three days later, they were laden down with presents for Jack. We got home at around 1 pm and Judith and Janet wanted to go 'shopping at the Coop'. While they were inside and Jack and I waited in the car, he told me that the argument was 'because of the drink' and he'd become afraid of both of them because of all the shouting and screaming. I was also bewildered by their sleep arrangements ...... Dick and Jack had single beds while Judith and Janet share a double.

The following day, was my day with Jack, but she was furious, especially when he said he wanted to go cycling. I'd already been to get her a box of wine and she still wasn't content. Now she wanted pork chops. She had no intention of eating them and this was just a spoiling tactic. Nevertheless, I whipped down to the COOP and was on my way back when my phone rang. It was Jack, frantically yelling that the house was on fire!

THE WEEK OF THE BLUE LIGHTS

Sunday 9th March

I raced home to see smoke billowing from the ridge tiles. Racing inside, I shouted to Judith to call the fire brigade, but she was so pissed, she couldn't even see the keys on the handset. She started running around like a headless chicken, so I got them both out of the house before rather stupidly, going back in and heading up the stairs to investigate. I was met with a thick ceiling of choking black smoke and couldn't see beyond it. I called the fire brigade myself and they arrived within seven minutes.

Together with our neighbours, we stood in the street, watching helplessly as, for all we knew, our house was about to burn down. And yet, as I stood with my arm around Jack, who was crying and shaking, a strange calmness settled on me. What more could happen? Was life really worth all this shit?

After around 30 long minutes, the firemen came out and the chief asked me to join him upstairs. The whole house reeked of smoke and everything was blackened ... walls, carpets, furniture .... He escorted me up the staircase, into the master bedroom and showed me the burned curtains at the window before asking whether anyone had been using a naked flame up there. Of course not! I'd just come back but no one in their right mind would deliberately set fire to anything. He shook his head in disbelief and left.

I decided to deal with the aftermath of the fire myself and spent the following 2 days mopping up water from the hoses and rigorously cleaning everything. However, the walls were now permanently black rather than the brilliant white I'd painted them when I extended the house from a 2-bedroom bungalow into a 3-bed, 2 reception room dormer. This had cost be twice what I'd paid originally but the beautiful house was well worth the result. Needless to say, that Judith didn't lift a finger to help with the clean-up and deliberately prevented work by continuously inviting a host of kids in.

Monday 10th March

Despite the excitement, the previous day, I noticed that there was only 1/3 of the box of wine left, meaning she'd drunk the equivalent of around 3 bottles after the fire brigade left.

I stayed at home until around 930am so that I could call the insurance company. As I left, Dick and Janet arrived. He asked if he could help, while she remained stoney silent. Then he took Jack and Judith to school where she told the headmaster what had happened. He suggested that she take the day off and she grasped the opportunity so that she and Janet could 'celebrate' together.

At 4pm Jack called to ask what time I'd be back. I said that I'd be earlier than normal because I had to start painting upstairs but was dropping in to see my mam on the way down. Because he'd been coached to repeat my words, Judith grabbed the phone and demanded that I get her some wine first. This meant passing my parents' house but I relented because I'd be too busy that night to be deflected by her tantrums. At 6pm I started painting. At 630pm she was screaming up at me to get more wine. I refused, telling her I was in the middle of painting when the physical threats began. While all this was going on, Jack had cut his finger and asked me to bandage it. Satisfying myself that it wasn't serious, I told him his mam would pop a plaster on it. She flatly refused unless I got her the wine. I was enraged and flew downstairs and demanded she got her coat on. Then the three of us drove to the COOP where I told her to buy her own wine.

Wednesday 12th March.

2am – the automatic alarm at work called my phone with an alert *'INTRUDER DETECTED…..INTRUDER DETECTED!'*.

I quickly dressed and raced to the workshop where I found we'd been burgled. In addition, the catalytic converter had been sawn off the main van. Most of the rest of the day was spent dealing with the police, repairing doors and getting the van repaired at some cost.

Saturday 15th March.

I'd decided to install CCTV at the workshop, I already had a system at home which Judith had demanded to keep an eye on 'other parents' who she suspected were stalking her. This, of course, was nonsense, so I thought it best to transfer it to work. In addition, I was going to install security lighting and dad volunteered to help me. By now, my mind was buzzing with all the week's events but I worked frantically to get the work done. All the while, Judith continually called me to pester for 'more wine!' She was really pissing me off.

At last, the final connection. I was preoccupied with her demands and impatient now. I was about to make a rash, life-changing decision.

The security light was high above me. I placed the ladders against the wall and found that dad wasn't around at that point to hold the bottom for me. I glibly thought it would be fine and climbed the 9 metres to the roof so I could complete the connection. I'd been working for around 2 minutes when the phone rang again. It was her – demanding that I left immediately and bring her wine. Needless to say, I was annoyed. Then, oddly, I saw the white breeze block interior wall rushing past my eyes. The sensation followed ... I was falling. Everything slowed to a crawl and time seemed to stop. I knew what was happening, of course and wondered *'how much more? What else!?'*

I was loudly interrupted by the crash as I hit the concrete floor. At first, I felt nothing but a warm sticky pool around my head. I'd fallen face first and, rolling over, I then suffered the searing pain. My left leg was caught between the rungs of the ladders, which were now bent at a right angle. My face had been burst open in a line from my left eye socket, down my nose and chin towards my throat. I couldn't see but could feel the raised black mounds where my eyes should be. Worst of all, for me, was that my teeth had gone. Those teeth which my mam had lovingly made sure were well cared for since I was an infant. I let as though I'd betrayed her.

I heard dad *"Oh what a bloody mess! What a bloody mess!"* he kept repeating. All I could do was lie there and cry *"How much more? .... How much more?!"*

Dad composed himself and called for an ambulance. Meanwhile, he started to mop up the blood, telling me not to move. I managed to lift my arm and wrap it around his legs, saying *"I'm sorry .... I'm sorry"*. I wanted him to know that it wasn't his fault but, more than that, I was sorry for the torment and misery I'd brought into to the family. I was deeply ashamed but the years of male restraint and distance between father and son had gone in seconds. Only one thing though ... in his eagerness to clean up the mess, dad had inadvertently used an old rag soaked in cellulose thinners to dab my facial wounds. For a brief moment, I thought I might end up back on the roof as the chemicals burned into my face.

The ambulance crew arrived within 15 minutes and I was checked for spinal injury before being strapped into a chair. In the ambulance, I asked for my phone which had miraculously survived, being one of those indestructible Nokias. I called home and did my best to speak through my toothless mouth to tell Jack everything was cool, but dad wouldn't be home for a while because I'd had a bit of an accident. Judith grabbed the phone and demanded that I get back now! *"And don't forget the wine!"*. I told her I was on the way to hospital, but she slammed the phone down and ran across the road to a neighbor's asking for help. She was hysterical. Wendy, the neighbour, called me but, by that point, I wasn't making much sense. All I could say was *"Is Jack OK?"*.

At Durham University Hospital, they decided that they couldn't do much for me other than clean me up, steristrip my face together and refer me to Newcastle RVI the following day. This was after I'd taken a 'selfie' which I have to this day to remind me that, I might not be handsome, but I'm sure as shit better than I looked then!

I limped out of hospital afterwards, trembling uncontrollably. Mam and dad collected me and dropped me home, preferring not to come in. Judith had sent Jack away with Dick and Janet. She screamed at my appearance and started to pat me in her drunken state. I crawled into the sofa bed in the dining room.

Sunday 16th March

Dick arrived with Jack. I wished he hadn't because my appearance both horrified and shocked the lad.

Dad collected me at 1145am and took me to the RVI where they literally glued my face back together. I knew I'd be marked for life but, at least, there'd be no stitching scars and I could therefore pretend to be a war hero rather than Frankenstein's creation. When I got home, I asked Judith to send Jack's friend home (he'd arrived just after I'd left for hospital) because they kept coming into the room to stare at me and that was more than I could bear. He'd been there the day of the accident, but she couldn't remember how he got home. It turns out it was the son of a neighbour who took him home when they found Judith drunk.

At around 6pm I asked Jack if he'd eaten. She hadn't fed him but had allowed his friend to scoff any amount of crisps, biscuits and sweets. She turned on Jack, raging at what he'd told me. Her face was filled with venom and she became very threatening. I thought she was going to hit him when she turned on me instead. She was on the point of doing so when she suddenly backed off and flew into the bathroom, slamming the door and leaving Jack in tears.

When she came out of the bathroom, she called for Jack and said she wanted to talk to him. Because she'd been so irate, I didn't want him to come to any harm so I kept him with me. Later, despite my state, she asked me to take them to the COOP to buy food for Jack and some things for his packed lunches. I couldn't see him go hungry and managed, with some difficulty to drive there although, truthfully, I shouldn't have done it because of the state of my eyes. I waited outside and they eventually emerged with two bottles of wine and comic for Jack. She then said she had enough food at home for him and, when we returned, she gave him a single bread bun with a slice of ham. I then found myself cleaning the kitchen which was in a terrible state. Jack wanted to go to bed on his own but she wouldn't allow it. He stayed with me and eventually drifted off. True to form, she then joined us and I had to drag myself upstairs to bed because I was too sore to share the sofa bed with them.

Monday 17th March

No Dick and Janet this morning so I managed to take Jack to school despite driving being very difficult and painful. He was extremely quiet.

I got back home and waited for the loss adjuster for the fire damage. I asked how Jack was getting home after school and she said that she'd get another parent to bring him home because she didn't want anyone seeing me in 'that state'. Her reasoning was that the other parents would wonder why SHE wasn't collecting him instead of me. I said that he'd had enough upset and that he ought to be picked up by someone in his own family, such as my mam and dad. At that she went off on another rant and started to shout and scream, just as the doorbell rang. She continued screeching at the loss adjuster when she opened the door and later had to apologise. Apparently, she'd not taken her meds for two weeks.

Later in the day, I had to get dad to take me to Sainsbury to shop for the week's groceries. I wore dark glasses to disguise my bulging eyes and use the trolley as a walking aid. While I was there, Judith called and asked me to collect her meds from the chemist … and also a bottle of wine. We dropped off the shopping, meds and booze before going off to collect Jack from school.

I knew the end was coming and my efforts to keep the family together were doing Jack more harm than good. Up to now, I'd convinced myself that he'd be better off with two parents than be a child from a broken home. I was wrong. The arguments, violence and outrageous behaviours were on the point of causing him permanent harm.

A few weeks later, I consulted a solicitor who advised me to seek a divorce on the grounds of Judith's unreasonable behaviour. However, he also told me to keep the account of her behaviour 'deliberately mild' so as not to provoke her too much. This may get a more speedy result and the court would otherwise regard a more detailed and explicit account as unnecessarily 'antagonistic'. They were likely to disregard it anyway as a factor in the divorce.

I needed time to think about what this all meant for Jack. I was inclined to fight for sole custody, to keep him safe from the antics of Judith and her parents. Of course, there'd be fair access but, by limiting Dick and Janet's influence, the situation could be brought under control. After that, there was the question of splitting the matrimonial assets which, thanks to them, were virtually nonexistent. They were, in fact, matrimonial debts. We would need to sell the house, pay off creditors and try to find some form of rented accommodation. Judith would need to pull herself around and either work or register for full benefits. If the business could still continue, I should be able to pay her a substantial amount in maintenance. In order to allow me to think all this through, it was agreed that a summary of the meeting would be mailed to my parents' address, along with a draft divorce proposal.

To my horror, the solicitor's office posted the bundle to our home address! I wasn't there when Judith opened it but to say she was livid is to vastly underplay it. By the time I got home, having 'obeyed her summons' she'd called my solicitor to contest every point. She'd also forced Jack to listen to the correspondence as she read it aloud. This made him very upset and then angry at me. While he was there, I wasn't going to discuss it and waited until he went to sleep before telling her that it was over. However, she continued to drink heavily and was extremely aggressive. Because of this and the upset that it had caused Jack, I decided that I couldn't proceed and asked the solicitor to put the matter on hold. I continued to soldier on, but life continued to deteriorate at the hands of both Judith and Janet, who made things increasingly miserable. I was approaching rock bottom.

BACK TO THE FUTURE AND THE DAY OF WINKLES

It was Friday, 24th March and I'd managed to return to work with some difficulty. However, my bulging black eyes were less horrific and I was walking, albeit with the aid of a stick. Driving was easier and, over the next four days, I pushed myself to the limit, trying to work through the backlog and keep on top of the situation at home.

That afternoon, I had three inspections to do, all spread out in Newcastle, Sunderland and, lastly, Washington at 5pm. I'd just left the first call when Jack telephoned me to say that his mam 'needed' some winkles. This was a clear sign that she'd been drinking heavily because her appetite for these types of flavours increased with her alcohol intake. I explained to him that I was on calls but he was becoming distressed and I could hear her in the background, shouting. I decided to make a slight detour and pass our house on the way to Sunderland, telling him I'd be there in 20 minutes or so. When I arrived, she was waiting for me, aggressive, shaking and out of control. She demanded that I go and get her a bag of winkles. I refused and told her I was now running late. She screamed *"I NEED WINKLES NOW!"*. She insisted I go back to Newcastle and buy them from the Green Market. This was impossible because the Green Market had been demolished several months earlier. I left the house after much arguing, but she was really kicking off. Her anger and aggression were about as bad as I'd seen before. I was very concerned for Jack so drove around the corner and called Social Services. I'd previously tried to get help from them without success, but the situation was out of control and urgent. It took an age to get through but, shortly before 5pm, someone eventually answered. I quickly summarised what had happened and their advice was to return home immediately to ensure Jack's safety. They also told me to call the police if things deteriorated and there was a direct threat to Jack. Of course, I'd had no intention of completing my calls but had used this as an excuse to leave the house to make this call. I was on the point of moving off when Jack called, scared to death *"Dad, you better get back, she's wrecking the house!"*

I was back within two minutes to be met by Jack at the door, his eyes wide and his face panic stricken. I ran in to see her sitting smugly on the floor. I warned her about her behaviour and told her what she was doing to Jack. She ranted and raved. Once again, it was getting out of hand so I told her I'd just called Social Services. Her face immediately changed into that of an evil, enraged, furious animal.

"STOP …. STOP IT! …. LEAVE MY DAD ALONE!".

A new determination took over. I had to tell him that I was OK… dad was OK …… everything would be OK. But he'd seen it all before … he'd heard it all before …. things no 8-year-old child should ever have to witness. I knew that this was it and it could go on no longer. My priority was him and to hell with the consequences, now. The time for cowardly, passive tolerance was over. I was ashamed, deeply ashamed, for what I'd allowed to become familiar.

"STOP IT NOW … I'LL KILL MYSELF!"

The pain was kicking in now, my heart was pounding and I was breathless and trembling. In that instant, though, I knew what to do. Darting past my attacker, I ran for the second door in the living room, knowing that they would follow my distraction. Circling back into the kitchen along the passage, I grabbed Jack and gathered him into my arms, forcing the knife from his small fingers which gripped it with unbelievable strength. I limped into the hallway and out of the front door, down the steps and into the garden. The escape attempt was frantic and agonising. I was in my late forties, overweight and unfit. My legs felt like lead and it seemed that I was hardly moving – like one of those nightmares where you're running from an unknown terror but making no progress. This terror, though, wasn't unknown, it was dreadfully well known to me.

There was no time to look for my keys and no time to waste in getting into my small van and starting it. We had to get out of there NOW. It was late afternoon but too early for any of the neighbours to be around. Most worked and weren't yet home. All we could do on that cold March Friday – was run!

In the street, I lowered Jack to his feet and grabbed his hand. Together we ran and didn't look back. We ran as fast as we could up that steep forbidding hill. Despite my injuries, I had to get him to safety. Heart pounding in my chest. Sweat running down the back of my neck, legs trembling and gasping for every breath, I pulled him by the hand. With his little feet padding behind me, I tried to reassure him that everything was going to be OK. His breathing was heavy as he whimpered pathetically – but not as pathetically as I felt! I was his dad, the one he looked up to, the one he came to for comfort. Now I was just a coward who'd betrayed him and failed to protect myself.

We reached the top of the hill and I looked back, relieved that we weren't being followed. We stopped for breath, but the terror wasn't over. Any minute now, Judith or her parents could appear and I was afraid that Jack would be snatched away. We ran a little, walked a little, ran a little for just over a mile until we reached the police station. We stumbled through the automatic door and into safety.

"I've been attacked!", I blurted to the desk officer who studied my bloodied and panicked face. He calmly took some details, signalled to some seats and, while we sat, he went off to find his sergeant. He returned quickly and told us that someone would be along very soon.

We sat in silence until *"Dad, I'm hungry"*. He seemed guilty at having to mention it and didn't want to add to the stress. The officer heard, came over to him and knelt down in front of him. Smiling at Jack he asked, *"How about a drink of pop and some chocolate for now?"*. Looking at me for reassurance, I nodded to Jack before he took the policeman's offered hand and disappeared into the canteen with him. My little boy looked like a hobbit in comparison to the towering officer and, yet I began to feel more at ease. This was an act of human kindness neither of us had felt for many years. That simple act of humanity lives with me even today. As trivial as it was, I felt tears welling up in my eyes. There were good people out there and we weren't alone. For a brief moment I started to recover my faith in people. This was to be short lived however when, only 3 days later, we were betrayed by those in authority who, supposedly, had a duty of care. For the moment, though, we were safe.

ON THE RUN

After around 10 minutes another officer arrived and introduced himself as the acting sergeant. We were led through some double doors, along a spartan corridor and into a small office containing a desk and two chairs. He invited me to sit, gave Jack the second chair and perched himself on the corner of the desk. I began to tell him the strange story which had started as a comedy and ended up in horror.

Jack was feeling a bit more at ease and was keen to put the record straight. *"I saw it all! .... I tried to help dad! .... I was going to kill myself!!".* I quietened him down and went through the sordid situation. I told of the repeated assaults and of the virtual hell Jack and I were living in.

"And your son saw all of this?"

"Yes! Yes!" Jack eagerly chipped in again.

The sergeant carried on, *"You need to understand that, if you make a formal complaint, we'll have to interview your wife under caution ... She could even be arrested!".* This time I didn't need to think for a second. The whole thing was out of control. He asked us to stay where we were while he and a colleague went off to interview Judith.

The next two hours seemed like an eternity.

Jack and I cuddled and talked, He asked what was going to happen to us, but I had no answers for him. Our little family group had been torn apart and all I could wonder aloud was about a new start, in a new home – just the two of us. He was all for that. He wanted to be safe, fed, loved and cared for – he wanted to be with his dad.

The sergeant returned having been to the house. By the time he'd arrived, Dick and Janet were there. Janet was warned about her drunken and aggressive manner. Judith was also hostile and uncooperative, so he'd been forced to arrest her and take her to the divisional headquarters in Gateshead, where she'd been put in a cell 'to cool off'. Eventually, she would admit the assault on me and agreed to accept a caution. She was then returned to the house we'd once known as 'home'.

"I'd strongly recommend that you keep yourself and your son away from your wife this weekend, for your own safety." The sergeant advised us *"You should call social services on Monday and ask for their help because we've done all we can really. We wouldn't like to see the boy back at home until you've spoken to social services. If you'd been the mother, we could have helped more by getting you to a place of safety. Unfortunately, there aren't any options for a father or any man for that matter".*

He then asked if we had anywhere we could

go. I explained that I could probably stay with my elderly parents but had no clothes or vehicle with me. I'd also left my pain killers, blood pressure and stomach medicines at the house. He volunteered to go back to the house to get some clothes and the meds. 15 minutes later, he returned from his mission of human decency. He didn't have to do that and I thanked him for it.

On leaving the station, I switched on my phone so that I could call my parents. I was greeted by a torrent of abusive voicemails from Judith, her mother and father. I called mam who was relieved to hear from us. She hadn't known what had happened of course, until she received a string of wild phone calls, accusing her of hiding us. Dad eventually arrived at the police station and we got into the car. I briefly tried to explain what had happened with Jack excitedly joining in. He stopped only to complain about being hungry. *"How about some of the best fish and chips in the world?!"*, Dad asked him. So off we went and then back to grandma and granddads' for tea.

By now it was 8pm and my parents' phone was ringing off the hook. At the start, mam had told them that she didn't know where we were. Then she started to stonewall them before trying to ignore the calls. After around the 20th time, Dad answered and was hit by a torrent of abuse from Dick. He demanded to know if he knew what his *'fucking son'* had done to his daughter by taking Jack away. Dad calmly asked if Dick knew what Judith had done to us!

I settled Jack into my old bed and he fell asleep as soon as his head hit the pillow. As the phone calls continued relentlessly, my rest was broken and tortured. So, dad and I sneaked back to the house and I nervously managed to start up my works van with a spare set of keys I kept at mam and dad's. No one saw us and, at least, now we had wheels.

What was going to happen to us? What should I do about Jack? What do I do about school on Monday? What do I do about clothes, the house, social services, the marriage, finances, work ...... when will the fucking phone stop ringing!?

The main problem at the moment was that weekend. The strain on my parents was telling on their faces and the threat of those maniacs turning up and causing real trouble was at the front of my mind. And then there was the effect it was all having on Jack. At 4 in the morning, the answer dawned as day broke – we had to run. Again!

Saturday 25th March

Mam and Dad were in their late 70s and in poor health. I had to relieve the stress on them and protect them.

I got showered early and ran a bath for Jack. We had to get out of the house because Judith and her parents might turn up at any moment, so we bundled ourselves into the van and headed for Jack's favourite breakfast – a McDonalds sausage and pancakes. The restaurant was less than a mile away but I felt safer, believing that they'd not think of looking for us there. Jack was chirpy and chatted about school and his friends, but not a word about his mother. I asked him if he wanted to go home but he was adamant. He didn't want to go back, he didn't want to see her and he didn't want to talk to her on the phone.

We left McDonalds and drove around the back of a nearby hotel so I could think my next move. Deciding I needed help, I switched on my phone to a deluge of voicemails .. drunken screams from Judith, threats from Dick and hysterical screeches from Janet. Once I cleared the messages, I nervously called directory enquiries and asked for the number for the social services department. My large fingers were more cumbersome than usual and I misdialed several times. Somehow, I got through and realised that directory enquiries had put me through to the emergency team based in Northumberland rather than the Gateshead team. This actually turned out to be a good thing.

Rather than have to explain the whole saga again, I asked the duty supervisor if she could consult the notes of 'the case' recorded by Gateshead. Disappointingly, she had no access to the notes and, as it was the weekend, wouldn't be able to speak to anyone at Gateshead. So it was that I had to trawl through the whole story for the umpteenth time. She then asked me for the contact number of the police sergeant who dealt with us the previous afternoon and said she'd call me back in a couple of hours.

We sat in the van and I did my best to keep Jack calm and occupied, playing 'eye spy' for ages. He loved that game, especially when he gave me impossible clues. He also asked me to tell him more of my made-up stories about the adventures of the big white van, the little white van and the little black 4x4, being our two works vehicles and his battery jeep. We shared a close and loving bond. By contrast, Judith never read to him or took an interest in who he was or what he achieved. Together with her parents, she saw him as a 'possession', 'THEIRS'. They suffocated him in 'things' but starved him emotionally.

I'd been ignoring and rejecting the calls that kept coming from home until an unfamiliar number appeared. It was the emergency team supervisor who'd now spoken to the police. On NO account was I to take Jack home. We had to stay away until Monday morning when they would immediately ask the Gateshead team to call me to discuss the next step. In the meanwhile, she said, *"Just be there for Jack and let him know you love him"*. Jack asked what she'd said. *"Good! I don't want to go back. You and me can be together!"*. He said as I began to feel overwhelmed. I sat for a while, pondering what to do before deciding that we needed to get out of the borough. Dick wouldn't drive around looking for us because that would be out of his comfort zone.

We had to last 2 days and all we had was what we were wearing. The first order of business, then was clothing and toiletries. I had no money on me and the credit cards were all maxed out. Fortunately, I still had £600 in the small account I'd set aside for Jack, so we drove into Durham and I was able to kit him out in a good selection of clothes and shoes from the Dalton Park Outlets centre. Next .. where to stay?

We headed for the coast. In Sunderland, I

pulled into a Brewers Fayre for lunch. I switched on the phone to check if there were any further messages from social services but all I got were 10 or more abusive messages, demanding I take Jack home. Judith was distraught and, despite what she'd done, I couldn't help feeling sorry for her. But my priority was Jack and I needed to keep him away until I got help. She had to confront her problem and, somehow, we had to get those two malicious controlling bastards out of our lives. I guess I must have asked Jack every 10 minutes if he wanted to speak to her, but he refused. It was *all her fault*. So, I decided to call Judith. She begged, threatened, pleaded and screamed. But while my heart ached for her, it was breaking for Jack. He was all that mattered now!

After lunch, we headed towards the riverside, the beach and then Marsden rock . He thoroughly enjoyed the day and seemed to detach himself from the horror of yesterday and the nightmare of the last few years. I marvelled at his spirit and wished I could be as strong.

In South Shields, we found a pleasant B&B to stay at. The welcome was warm and we were given the biggest suite they had. It had a massive array of books and DVDs and Jack watched 'Ice Age', belly laughing all the way through. It made me happy and proud. We had a nice evening meal at a local Italian restaurant where Jack ate with enthusiasm and was very taken with a blue plastic seal they served his ice cream inside. He kept it and treasured it for months. At the B&B and after bedtime stories, he fell asleep with his arm draped over my chest. He was peaceful.

I gently got off the bed and went over to an armchair where I switched-on my phone. More abuse, wailing and gnashing of teeth. I telephoned my mother and found that they'd had to leave their own house because of the constant calls and abuse from Judith and her parents. I hadn't told her where we were at that stage and she didn't want to know either. That way, she'd have nothing to tell anyone. All she wanted was to know that we were safe. I assured her we were.

Sunday 26th March

Breakfast! Jack and I were the only guests and the landlady made a great fuss over him. She asked what had brought us there at that time of year. And so, out of Jack's hearing, I shared. Ironically, she had a sister who was an alcoholic and she knew our heartache well.

We spent the day walking along the seafront and on the beach, building sandcastles and pyramids. Jack was having a whale of a time and told me he loved being with me *'because we did things'*. That night, we stayed in a hotel on the outskirts of Gateshead and prepared for the call from social services in the morning. That phone call never came ...

Monday 27th March

I called Jack's school to explain his absence. Jack's teacher, who I'd met at a parents' evening, told me that she'd been worried about him for some time. He was becoming increasingly withdrawn and dark. She told me about a 'show and tell' morning when Jack had shocked her and his classmates. The other children had shown off their books or toys and talked about them. Jack told them about the day he 'nearly' had a baby brother or sister, but his mam had told him that his dad made her 'put it in a bucket and flush it down the toilet'! The other kids were distressed and the teacher was appalled. I couldn't comprehend why she'd said such a thing to him and I was filled with disgust and horror.

It was now 11am and I was concerned that the message to Gateshead social services

hadn't been received. So, I decided to call
them.

FALSE PROPHETS

Long before the events of that weekend, I'd asked for help from social services. Judith's alcoholism was spiralling out of control, her mood swings were extreme and she was increasingly violent towards me. At this stage I wasn't aware of her hitting Jack or just how afraid of her he REALLY was. Her behaviour was getting more bizarre by the day. I genuinely didn't know how to handle the situation. I'd been to get help from Relate; Alanon; The Oasis Project, Northeast Council on Addictions and my local PCT but nobody seemed able to offer practical and meaningful help. All I got was - *'stop allowing her the means to feed her habit'* - or *'get out of the marriage'*. The first was easier said than done and the second was out of the question. I couldn't leave, although God alone knew how I longed to get away from this torture. I had to stay and cope for the sake of my son. If I left and took him with me, we would surely be hunted down and the backlash would be beyond imagination.

As the situation had become dire, I'd called social services the previous November to ask for an appointment. The duty officer explained that they *'didn't really do appointments'* and asked me why I wanted to see them. I briefly explained and was curtly advised to call-in and ask for the duty officer if I wanted to. So, I went, reported to the desk and asked to see the duty social worker. After half an hour's wait, I was ushered into a side office. Susan Taylor introduced herself and asked me what I wanted to discuss. I was well prepared and had written down all my concerns and approached the situation calmly and logically, trying to package-up our family dilemma in digestible 'boxes'. I explained that I was there for the sake of my son and that I was desperately worried for his physical and emotional well-being. I told her what steps I'd previously taken to tackle the nightmare we were living and how I'd tried to manage Judith's drinking problem, how I protected Jack, how I was trying to manage an unmanageable situation. I listed the agencies I'd turned to and described the magnitude of Judith's drinking problem, the violence, the use of Jack as a weapon against me, the control, the isolation, the influence of Judith's parent, the fact that Jack was being neglected when I wasn't around, the obsession with him and the sleeping with him by both Judith and her parents (Judith often naked). I even re-counted comments Judith had recently made to me about her being sexually abused as a child - albeit (she claimed) by the grandfather of a friend. She'd also told me her mother had asked her whether her father had ever 'touched' her. All of these concerns added up to a serious situation which justified some involvement by the department.

Susan Taylor asked what I wanted social services to do about 'it'. (What did she mean by - 'IT"? - we weren't an 'IT", we were a family going through hell). I drew breath and told her that I needed help to cope, Judith needed help and Jack needed support.

Her response stunned and appalled me. *"We don't normally deal with people like you"* she said in a matter-of-fact tone. *"We're used to dealing with people from the poorer areas of the borough not middle-class families like yours. Jack is obviously loved - despite your concerns over the way he's loved. Why are you complaining about the woman who has brought up your son - are you just having a bad day?"*

I was speechless. It was an arrogant, sexist and prejudiced statement posed as a 'question'. She was effectively telling me that I'd had no part part in raising Jack and that I was a moaning, good-for-nothing man. I may have provided the sperm - but that's all I'd brought to fatherhood. Her assumption was that it was Judith who had 'brought up Jack'. NO! - I was a loving father who needed, demanded to be heard. I wasn't simply the bloke who happened to live in the same house. I was DAD - I cared for and supported this child physically and emotionally, protected him against his mother's onslaughts, nurtured him, entertained him and educated him. Whenever he was sad or ill - it was ME he turned to. Did all of this count for NOTHING? In that brief moment, the hostility and prejudice against me were starkly clear. I left feeling further isolated and alone. Who do I turn to now?

Judith's behaviour and the controlling of her parents continued. I'd made further calls to social services but the outcome was the same. On that previous Friday in March, knowing full well what I would be walking into - I called them again to plead for help. Inconveniently, it was nearly 5pm. I was told that if I thought Jack was in danger, then I should take him out of the house - and call them on Monday. It was if I'd caught the doctor at a difficult moment to be told "take a couple of aspirin and call me in the morning".

Monday March 27th – present day.

I waited until 11 am and no call came. I decided to call them. I thought, things would be different. This time, the police had been involved and their own colleagues had even told me to keep Jack away. This time - they had to help ....How wrong I was.

I got through and was passed to the officer dealing with the case. My heart sank as I discovered that this was Ms. Taylor again. She claimed that she'd been trying to call me. This was a lie - my phone had been switched-on and available all morning. She insisted that I took Jack back to his mother despite me protesting that she didn't understand. I told her what had happened and was shocked to hear her deny that she'd had any contact with the police or the emergency team. If that was the case - why did she claim that she was trying to call me? Eventually, she did agree to meet us at the civic center.

The drive through the traffic to Gateshead was one of the longest journeys of my life, even if it was only 5 miles. Jack and I talked about what was happening. I told him that, if they asked him anything, he should simply tell the truth about what had happened and how he felt.

We arrived at Social Services. Ms. Taylor appeared and asked to see Jack - alone. After about 5 minutes they emerged from the office. She flattered him and commented on what a bright and intelligent boy he was — *"now take him home to his mother!"* I protested yet again, but she'd hear none of it and told me that she had other work to attend to. If I was so worried about Jack - it was for me to *seek legal advice and remove him from home*. With those comments ringing in my ears, we left, neither of us saying much. She just didn't get it, I was trying to repair the family, not break it apart! Why wouldn't she help? I was bewildered and approaching rock bottom. Why would no-one believe me?

I decided that I couldn't take Jack back immediately. We were hungry and confused. We drove to my parents' and mam fed us before Jack disappeared into the garage to get some toys to play with. At that moment, my world fell-apart. I wept - aloud. I ran to Jack and cuddled him - I felt that this was the last time I would see my son.

After lunch, we returned to the dreaded place called 'home". Judith ran out to greet Jack and smothered him with kisses and cuddles. She was hysterical. Her mother and father did the same. I went into the house and sat alone in the study and allowed them to do what they had to do. Inside me, though, something major had changed. I realised that there was no longer a place for me there. I was unwelcome in my own home. It was legally my house but I'd lived at one end of it for the last 3 years because I couldn't bear to share the same space as that despicable trio. I now realised that this was their house. Janet and Dick had succeeded in forcing me out by 'squatting' there for the past 8 years. Now, they'd also succeeded in prising my son away from me.

After a few days and a great deal of agonising, I knew that the game was finally up. I knew that there was no future. I couldn't stay because of the atmosphere in the home, the arguments and the violence were making Jack's life unbearable. I'd tried to tough-it-out and stay, so that I could be there to ensure his safety and happiness. I'd failed and, by doing what I thought was best for him, had added to his desperate situation and his unhappiness. As long as I was around, he'd be used as a weapon against me and alienated from all that I wanted for him. I could stay and fight and see him further distressed and damaged .....or I could go and at least hope that he would find peace. I knew I had to leave.

I sat him on my knee and told him what I needed to do. He became hysterical, ran into the hall and buried his head in the coat rail. I rushed to him and we hugged, both crying. Judith screamed abuse at me and told me I was hurting Jack. – *"JUST GO"*. I wept and shook with rage and frustration. I wanted her and her parents to die, I wanted to hurt them so badly, I wanted justice, I wanted revenge. But, more than all of that, I wanted

Jack to find peace. He'd often said to me –
"Dad - I don't have a very nice life". So, I walked
out of the front door and down the drive
into the van. Turning the ignition on, I
numbly glanced back to the door. There he
stood …. my angelic, beautiful boy, tears
streaming down his cheeks … waving 'bye
bye' to dad!

CALM BEFORE THE STORM

Things died down for a few days. Judith was relieved to have Jack home and she called me to say she wanted to make a fresh start. I told her I needed to think but returned to the house to carry on redecorating after the fire. She wanted me to come back permanently but was still drinking heavily. I continued to stay with mam and dad and turned my thoughts towards how our family could survive.

I knew the marriage couldn't survive while she continued to drink heavily. I was prepared to do all I could to help her but, in the end, it was down to her. She had to WANT to stop and she had to go into rehab.

We couldn't survive as a family under the damaging influence of Dick and Janet. They should have the same access as any other 'normal' grandparents but their 24/7 presence and controlling behaviour had to stop.

If we were to survive as a normal family, the bad mouthing of my parents had to stop and they had to be allowed the same access as Dick and Janet. The deliberate alienation wasn't right and it was putting Jack under too much pressure.

Other things had to change to ... the out-of-control spending, the emotional suffocation of Jack, Judith's laziness and lack of contribution to parenthood and the household.

Because my mind was all over the place, I foolishly wrote all this down on a piece of paper before going to see Judith. I'd told her I wanted to talk to her, alone. We chatted amiably enough for a couple of hours and, to my surprise, she agreed with me, even admitting that Dick and Janet had ruined our relationship. So, we hugged and I went upstairs to continue decorating. At 6pm I packed up, removed my decorating shirt and jeans, got dressed and returned to my parents' house where I made plans to move back to my own home. The following day, however, the balloon went up.

Stupidly, I'd left my 'list' in the back pocket of my decorating jeans where Janet found it as she went on one of her fishing expeditions. By the time I got to the house, the shit had hit the fan. Judith's attitude had changed totally and I was accused of playing mind games and taking Jack away from Dick and Janet. She made it clear that 'the deal was off'!

The game was finally up. There was no going back and there was no future for us. For the second time in as many days, I left.

LOSING JACK – PART ONE

Over the coming weeks and months, I stayed at my parents' but continued to fully support my family by financing the house and all the bills. I did all the shopping, delivered it and even put it away in the cupboards. I gave Judith money and still continued to pay her credit cards.

Judith and I agreed that I would collect Jack from school each Friday afternoon and return him to her the following Sunday evening. This way, I could concentrate on earning a living to provide for us all during the week and spend quality time with him at weekends.

Over the next 2 months, he and I spent many great weekends together. In fact, we did many things we hadn't had the chance to do before. I tried very hard to entertain him and stimulate his interests. We visited fun fairs and museums, saw waterfalls, went fossil hunting and camping, did pottery, toured the Jorvik Centre in York and took part in some archaeology. We talked and bonded even further. In growing ever closer, Jack and I looked forward to each weekend as a new adventure.

Things then started to go wrong.

Judith complained that I never gave her

enough money. Initially, I gave her between £200 and £300 per week but found that there was still no food in the house and Jack was deprived of essentials. Following the advice of my solicitor, I stopped giving her money and started to do the shopping myself. I still gave her around £100 per week but she saw this as a way of controlling her. Before long, she and her parents were complaining bitterly that I could take Jack on 'all these adventures' but they couldn't afford to do the same. When I suggested that they used the money they spent on alcohol instead, their reaction was furious.

There was bitter resentment over my relationship with Jack. At first, there was criticism and name-calling. Then I found that 'other arrangements' had been made for Jack's weekends. When I did get access, we were plagued with up to 10 phone calls a day from Judith and her parents, asking whether he was OK and demanding to know what he was doing. He was told they were 'missing him', that 'his friends' had been to the door asking for him, he was told that they had presents waiting for him ....

One Saturday, I decided to take Jack to the Northumberland coast. Against my wishes, he'd stayed with Judith at her parents the night before, when he should have been with me. However, I collected him on the way up and we spent an enjoyable time in Seahouses and Bamburgh, took a boat trip around the Farne Islands and saw a school of dolphins. They called and spoke to him repeatedly during the day, I guess on about 9 occasions. We travelled back towards home and took-in an adventure playground on the way. When we got home, and after tea, we decided to go to the cinema and spent a couple of hours watching a movie. My phone was switched off in the theatre as is usual. After the showing, I switched-on the phone and was shocked to receive a voicemail from Whickham police who'd already tried to contact me via my parents! I returned the call immediately and we were shocked to be told that Judith and her mother had been to the police station accusing me of abduction. They told the police that they hadn't been able to contact him and hadn't spoken to him for a couple of days. They were extremely concerned for him. The officer asked whether Jack was with me and if he was OK. She asked where I'd been with him and why I hadn't allowed his mother and grandparents to speak to him. I told her that we'd been out for the day and that Jack had been with them only yesterday. I also informed her that they'd spoken to him many times that day. She advised me not to 'worry' and that she was satisfied at what I'd told her. She confided that Judith and Janet were 'worse the wear for drink'! but, while she may have been satisfied, Jack and I were very shaken by the allegations and the involvement of the police.

That wasn't the only time Judith or her parents had called the police. On returning Jack home one Sunday evening, I was approached by a neighbour who told me that Judith had been 'helped' into the house only minutes before we arrived by a 'yobbish' looking young man. She was very drunk and they were still in the house. I decided not to expose Jack to this and took him to my parents. I asked my Mam to feed him while I went back to the house to investigate. I didn't want him to be walking into a nasty situation. As I approached the house, the youth was leaving in front of me. I recognised him as the son of one of Judith's 'friends'. I walked into the house and couldn't see Judith at first before finding her slumped in the office chair, asleep and obviously very drunk. The room had been wrecked. Rather than wake her, I wrote her a note to tell her that I'd be keeping Jack overnight because of her 'condition' and then left.

After tea, I drove with Jack to a shop to buy supplies for his packed school lunch the following day. The phone rang and a very angry Judith was on the line, demanding to know what I'd done with him. I told her what I'd seen and why I was keeping him for another night. She'd been in no condition to care for him. Her parents were now at the house and she'd put the conversation on speakerphone. Dick grabbed the phone off Judith and threatened to "*knock [your] fucking head off!*" He bellowed *"fetch that bairn back now!"* I refused and ended the call, but Jack was very upset at the way his granddad had spoken to me.

I settled Jack to bed at around 830pm. It was difficult getting him to sleep but, eventually, he drifted-off at around 9pm. At 920pm, the doorbell rang. I was still upstairs with Jack because he'd asked me to stay with him. My mother came upstairs and whispered that the police were at the door because Judith's parents had reported me for abduction! I invited the police officers in and explained the day's events. However, they insisted that they had a duty to satisfy themselves that Jack wasn't in any danger and we had to wake him. They spoke to Jack alone, upstairs. Eventually, they satisfied themselves that he was OK and left to return to see Judith and her parents and inform them that they could take no further action.

I took Jack to school the following morning

and, as usual, Dick collected him in the afternoon to take him back to Judith.

After these episodes, my access to Jack was savagely restricted. They often stopped him seeing me or demanded that I return him early. Any time my phone was off while he was with me, this was another nail in the coffin of my contact with him. On our visit to the Jorvik Centre in York (which was underground), there was no phone signal and they'd again tried to call Jack throughout the 45 minutes we were inside. When we got out and could be contacted again, they insisted we returned immediately. I refused, saying that we had every right to be together. I was told that Jack was theirs, not mine!

After several months, I was forced to stop paying several household bills as Judith and her parents abused the facilities and I ran out of money. They were running up telephone bills of in excess of £200 per month and I had to arrange for the account to be stopped so she could transfer it to her own name. I did provide Jack with a mobile phone, so that I could speak to him during the week and vice versa. Gradually, despite the fact that I was paying for it. the phone was switched-off and it was increasingly difficult to speak to him.

After we'd been camping on the weekend

after Jack's 9th birthday, contact stopped. I wasn't able to speak to him directly and the excuse was usually that he was with someone else, or at his grandparents. I continued to try to speak to him and once even went to his school and chatted with him through the fence at break time - much to the annoyance of Judith and her parents. One Tuesday evening in July, I managed to get a response from his phone, but it was Judith who answered. I asked to speak to Jack but she refused to let me. Eventually, she admitted that she'd sent him to one of his friends' houses a few streets away. She said that I should go there if I wanted to see to him before demanding to know *why* I wanted to see him. I said, "*because he's my son*". I drove to Jack's friend's house and knocked at the door but there was no answer so I then drove to our own house to find it in darkness. I decided to try his friend's house again. It was getting dark but, as I approached, I could clearly see Jack and his friend being bundled into the back of a car! I drove-up behind them but they sped-off. All I could see in the beam of my headlights was Jack's bewildered little face staring out of the rear window as he disappeared into the distance.

I rang Judith and she admitted she'd telephoned the other parents and had them drive Jack away to stop me seeing him. She didn't explain why she'd done it. I yelled *"HE'S MY SON and I had every right to see him!"* I put the phone down on the wicked bitch, pulled to the side of the road and wept for a while. I then returned to my parents. That was the last time I was to see my boy for 5 months.

WHILE THE CAT'S AWAY

I knew that Judith had taken a boyfriend a couple of weeks after I'd left the house. He was a lifeguard at the local swimming baths and used to visit the home regularly, often late at night. This relationship lasted only a short while.

Her drinking and behaviour didn't improve. Neighbours told me that, on one occasion at 4am Jack and a friend, who was sleeping over that night, had to call an ambulance themselves because she'd had another 'turn'. She continued to drink and drive with Jack and other kids in the car. This was brought to an abrupt end in late August 2008.

At 7 am on 23rd August, I was woken by a phone call from Gateshead police. They asked me if I knew where my car was. I told them I presumed it was on the drive of our property and that my wife was the main user. I was then told that it had been stopped the previous evening 12 miles from our home. It was being driven by a man with a 12-year-old girl inside. He was drunk, had been disqualified from driving and driving without insurance. He'd been arrested and held at the police station. I was shocked to say the least. I sent a text to Judith *"Where's my car?"*. The response was terse *"The police already told you"*. I asked again *"Where is it?"*.

There was no reply.

I asked my friend, Dave, to run me to the police station where I was given the keys and told where to find it. Neither Jack or Judith were involved in the incident and the car was OK. The man (Luke) was Judith's new boyfriend and by all accounts, an alcoholic and drug user. A later report about the incident in the local paper said he escaped a prison sentence because he was the carer for his three children! Dave and I drove to Birtley in County Durham, where I collected the car and delivered back home without going in to see Judith.

Judith and Luke's tribe managed to trash our house. He'd also broken down our back door with a sledgehammer when he'd tried to get to her. The neighbours had seen this but, somehow, Judith got Jack to 'admit' to me that he'd done it! Neighbours reported all night booze fuelled parties and kids hanging out of upstairs windows in the early hours. Taxis came and left at all hours. One day, a neighbour contacted me to tell me that the house was empty but the front door was wide open. I went down and what I saw disgusted me and made me physically sick. The house, my beautiful home, was wrecked and a slum. There were cannabis joints all around, spilled booze, cat shit and vomit, human vomit, dishes unwashed for weeks, mounds of dirty clothes and the garage was full of Luke's stuff.

Over the next few months, I heard little about Jack or how he was. I made constant attempts to contact him by phone and by text, without success. His phone was always switched off. I was still paying to maintain the house and all the bills but money was now very tight and business was bad. Apart from the telephone, other household bills were soaring. The June gas and electricity account was the thick end of £800. I wrote to Judith and insisted that she had to start to pull her weight, at least by claiming some form of benefit. Under the advice of my lawyer, I stopped buying groceries and instead, worked out an appropriate amount of money to pay to her, by transfer into her bank. Even though I was paying all the household expenses, car insurance and other bills, I calculated a generous allowance. I'd previously reported the break-up to the Child Support Agency and asked them for a ruling on how much to pay to her for Jack. I'd used their on-line calculator and came up with a figure. They eventually calculated what I should pay but, by then, I'd already been paying more and stuck to that, instead. She was also entitled to benefits and child allowance. At a total of £220 per week, I was more than confident that she could manage to adequately cater for herself and Jack.

On a few occasions, I bumped into neighbours and heard stories of continuing partying and drinking and a stream of people coming and going. It was a depressing and difficult time. I was angry and frustrated. I often went to sleep holding a photo of Jack. I spoke to him in my heart and cried a great deal. Without him, life had no meaning. I went through the routine of daily life, but I was dead inside. I would have given anything, paid any price, just to be able to talk to him. However, by directly stopping me seeing him and by alienating him from me, Judith and her parents succeeded in keeping my son out of my life.

JACK DISAPPEARS

Throughout the Summer and Autumn, I never gave up trying to contact Jack. I called his phone at least 3 or 4 times a day but it was always switched off. There was no reason for it to be off other than because his mother and grandparents made sure of it. Strangely though, his call costs were very high but the itemised bills proved that it was Judith who was making full use of it. From Jack, however, there were no calls - or even texts.

In late September. I discovered that a Dr Who exhibition was to be held over a weekend in Lanchester. Jack was a Dr Who fan and I knew he would want to go if only I could contact him. Finally, on 10th October, he answered his phone! Trying to hold back my emotions and tears, I briefly chatted with him about how he was and how he was doing. The conversation was strained and I knew someone was sitting over him, listening. I told him about the exhibition and asked if he would like to go with me. His answer shocked and appalled me - and raised a hundred questions.

"Well - as you know - Mam's in hospital!" he replied in a matter-of-fact way.

I was speechless and silent for what seemed an age.

"Are you there Dad?"

"Yes, yes son! - what are you talking about? I don't know about this - what's happened?" I blurted.

"She's in hospital with a tummy ache" he said

"When did this happen?"

"A few weeks ago" was his answer

"Well - where are you???? Who's looking after you??"

"I'm at grandma and granddad's"

"Why wasn't I told then ....what's going on?"

"I don't know Dad, I thought they'd told you!"

"Look, we'll leave it at the moment but promise me you'll leave your phone switched-on. I'll need to talk to some people and I'll need to speak to you again - OK?"

"Well they didn't ... ... OK Dad .... Bye"

"I love you son"

I ended the call and sat dazed, wondering what had happened to Judith, what had happened to Jack, what I should do next.......
I decided that the first thing I needed to do was visit the house and see if I could get any clues from there.

I drove home and walked in through an unlocked door. The state of the house was worse than ever. Lights and heating were blazing; there was rotting food all around; cold dirty and green tinged water in the bath ...

I went back out of the front door and sat on the step, head in hands. Then, I heard a friendly voice calling to me - it was one of the neighbours. She came over and I showed her the house. She was equally shocked and disgusted. By talking to her, I was able to piece together what had happened.

Two weeks earlier, two ambulances and a paramedic had suddenly appeared at the house. Dick and Janet were also there. Judith was rushed into hospital and Jack had been taken away by his grandparents. The story put around by Dick and Janet was that she'd had 'stomach' problems.

Sometime after my conversation with Jack, Judith called me from hospital. Her parents had told her that I'd managed to speak to him. She sounded tired, weak and confused - but still hostile. She warned me to stay away from Jack and blamed me for putting her in hospital by stopping paying for bills and not giving her enough money for food.

It didn't take me very long to decide on a course of action. My priority was to get Jack back. I didn't know what kind of hell he'd been through. I tried to suppress my rage and hatred of his grandparents for abducting him and deliberately hiding the truth from me, but I was going to need some cooperation from them until I got Jack back. First, I had to provide a safe, clean and secure home for him. I had to get my house back, but Dick and Janet were making free use of the place. They'd had a key for years. Therefore, the first thing I did was to change the locks and it didn't take long for the shit to hit that fan either. After I'd changed them. I left to buy cleaning materials. When I got back, neighbours told me that Dick and Janet had been and had tried to get in. Dick was heard to shout *"He's changed the locks!"* and with that, sped off out of the street. That afternoon, I received a text from Jack asking why I'd done it. I called him and explained that I did it because I didn't know who'd been using the house or who was coming and going. I could hear Dick and Janet in the background, telling him what to say to me. I told him that he should be with me at this time. There was a long silence and he eventually said he didn't really like the house! I told him I'd call back later.

The next step was to clean the place thoroughly. My dad and I spent 5 solid days tidying, disinfecting and cleaning. We made the place habitable and managed to get rid of the foul smells which had been lingering there.

The day after my second conversation with Jack, I received a call from Judith's father. The three of them had just left the hospital, having been told that Judith was dying! He was obviously distressed and mentioned that her liver was failing. He snapped that he intended to consult a solicitor and the police saying that he held me responsible for Judith's condition because I had 'cut everything off'. I didn't argue because I didn't want to add to his distress. I asked to speak to Jack and, to my surprise, this was allowed. He seemed to be handling the matter well, telling me he was a *'bit sad'* but otherwise sounded fine. I told him that he should be with me and he said he would probably see me that weekend.

That evening, I went to visit Judith at the hospital. I was deeply shocked at what I saw. She was in a coma having suffered liver failure. The consultant told me that this was alcohol induced and there was a very high chance she wouldn't survive. He said, if her kidneys failed, they wouldn't attempt to resuscitate her. Her skin was yellow, but not as yellow as the 'whites' of her eyes which contrasted against the cold and dead greyness of her irises. The only comparison I can make for this dreadful sight, is the eyes of dead fish as they lie on the fishmonger's slab. I stayed by her bedside and held her hand. I was overcome with pity, talking to her and stroking her hair. I stayed with her for a couple of hours, willing her to wake-up. This was a ritual I was to repeat over and again.

Jack wasn't allowed to see me that weekend despite having said that he would. I managed to speak with him on a couple of occasions though and offered to take him away for a few days during the coming half term holiday. He was very keen and I heard him ask his grandparents if it would be OK for him to go with me. He then told me it would be alright but only if I took him back when we returned. I also heard them telling him to ask for new clothes. I managed to force myself to speak to Janet. It was a civil conversation, but she told me that Judith's condition had worsened again and was grave. However, she thought that a few days away would be good for Jack and we agreed that they should drop him at home the following Wednesday lunchtime when they would be travelling to the hospital.

Wednesday lunchtime came. They arrived and Jack got out of the car. I was startled by how much he had grown - but he appeared pale and skinny too. Dick stayed at the bottom of the driveway and bellowed,

"Mind - when can we pick the bairn up again!?"

I stifled the rage that was welling up inside me. How dare that self-righteous, child abducting bastard?! I managed to keep control for Jack's sake and said I would call when we returned. I'd planned to take him to Alton Towers with his cousin, Katherine. If either they or Judith had found out, there would have been hell to pay but he needed to mix with my side of the family. Katherine would have no problem in keeping him company on the rides and other entertainment.

We left on our long journey. Jack was happy and smiling. I hadn't told him where we were going and he spent at least an hour excitedly guessing and interrogating me. It was a laugh. During the journey, Dick repeatedly called Jack. We could all hear what he was saying because I had linked his phone to my hands-free system. It was ironic because he called him on the same phone they had made sure was switched-off for me. Dick kept telling the lad that his mother was *'very, very poorly!'* While I had every sympathy with him, this was yet more self centred and cruel manipulation. Jack then told me he wanted to live with me after we got back home but was worried about what his grandparents would do.

The next three days were a blast for all of

us. Jack thoroughly enjoyed himself. Strangely, he didn't mention his mother once. If I asked if he wanted to call his grandparents (if they weren't calling him) but he refused.

When we returned on Sunday, we called at ASDA for groceries. Dick called again and spoke to Jack:

"Hello son - just to let you know that your Mam's very ill and she's dying. It'll be any time now!"

I was horrified at what he said but didn't want to upset Jack by blasting Dick, or for that matter, adding to his own pain. I ended the call by saying we'd call again later. I asked Jack how he felt. Again, he said he was *'a bit sad'* but was *"happy to be back with you Dad"*. I was relieved at how calmly he was taking all this, but his matter-of-fact reaction niggled at me too.

That evening, I called Dick and Janet to tell them that Jack would be staying with me now. Her reaction was more restrained than I imagined but, then again, she had other things on her mind. I really thought I'd got away with this one.

I settled Jack into bed at 830. At 910pm, there was a heavy knock at the door. Once again, it was two policemen. Jack got out of bed and came into the living room. He was wide eyed and afraid. The sergeant announced that Judith's parents had made allegations against me.

The officer was very helpful and understanding. He'd read the background notes to the case and, while he was talking to me, his colleague spoke to Jack.

Dick and Janet had alleged that Judith's alcohol addiction was the result of years of domestic violence on my part. They'd 'raised general concerns' about Jack's physical safety and emotional welfare while he was with me. They said that the home was scruffy and that I'd prevented Jack from having contact with them. The sergeant was obviously satisfied that what they said was untrue and said, *"Look - I'm not a sergeant for nothing! I know what's been going on, but I have a duty to follow-up any allegations when they involve a child. I'm going to go back and advise Mr. and Mrs. Harris that it's for them to seek a court order for custody if they feel Jack's at risk. However, as far as I'm concerned, he's safe and well - and wants to be with you"*

Jack was extremely upset but very angry. He said he didn't want to see his grandparents again. With that, the officers left.

This had all been cruel; malicious, unnecessary and manipulative. It was also harassment, let alone slanderous. It was

Dick and Janet who'd actively helped to block my access to Jack over the past few months and I was outraged. The sergeant had advised that as a matter of procedure, he had to draw the allegations they'd made to the attention of social services. Now that I was looking after Jack, I fully expected the department to come down on me like a ton of bricks.

I'd now run out of any remaining sympathy for Dick and Janet. I had to stop this campaign of theirs and I certainly didn't want Jack to have any further exposure to them until the matter was resolved.

At lunchtime on Monday, Jack's headmaster called me to say that he had found him in a highly distressed state in the assembly hall. He'd taken him into the office and asked him what was wrong. Jack told him what had happened the previous evening. The head was appalled and asked me if I would come to see Jack. I went immediately and decided to take him home for the rest of the day.

Over the next week, Jack settled back into school and made good progress. Despite the last week's fright, he was very happy and comfortable with me. He made it clear that he wanted to stay and have no contact with his grandparents. However, they continued to leave messages for him and even contacted his school to ask if they could visit him there. The headmaster informed me that he'd told them that it would be inappropriate. That evening, I called Janet and told her I would again ask Jack if **he** wanted to call **them**. I told her that I personally saw a role for them sometime in the future but that it was Jack who had decided that he didn't want to see or speak to them, not me! I told them that they'd caused this. Janet didn't argue and I ended the call.

Jack gradually began to reveal many disturbing things about his time with his mother and grandparents including violence and verbal abuse. I firmly believed it would be wrong at that time, for him to have access to any of them. Meanwhile, Judith's condition had miraculously improved. She remained in intensive care but was no longer on a ventilator. She was conscious. If she did get released from hospital she would need care, presumably at her parents. I believed that, if and when she recovered, there would be a great deal of trouble and anguish for Jack. The pressures they would put on him to go back to them would be immense and this was exactly what he didn't need.

Over the next few weeks, Jack and I settled into a normal routine. I arranged my working day around him, ran the house, fed him, put-up his packed lunches, did the washing and ironing, took him to school, collected him in the afternoons, made his tea, helped him with his homework,

entertained him and put him to bed. I shopped, cleaned and planned active weekends with him. Of course, I was also running a business too. This was tough and exhausting, but rewarding and enjoyable. It wasn't long before neighbours and the school were all remarking on the improvement in Jack's manner, appearance and well-being.

Money was a growing problem as the debts continued to mount and the business struggled. I even contemplated renting-out the house to get extra money and then rent a smaller place for the two of us.

Judith was continuing to recover. She was now putting pressure on Jack to go to see her in hospital and stay with her when she eventually left. She even threatened that she would return home when she was discharged. I told her that I wouldn't live under the same roof as her. Jack was adamant that he wanted to remain with me and was very reluctant to visit her either in hospital or at her parents' home. I began to build a case for Jack remaining with me on a permanent basis, for my lawyer. Jack even insisted on putting his own thoughts down on paper and drew up a sheet with two columns - one listed the reasons to stay with Dad and the other - why not to live with Mam! At no time, though, did I talk negatively to him about either his mother or grandparents. I, for one, was not going to involve him in a 'war' between us or involve him in 'grown-up' affairs.

In early December, I managed to persuade Jack to visit Judith in hospital. He wasn't happy about it and was very reluctant. I genuinely believed she needed to see him and he ought to see her. She was already accusing me of deliberately withholding him from her. I'd visited her on my own a few days earlier. She'd instructed the hospital staff not to discuss her condition with me and demanded I give her £300. On this occasion, I decided that I wouldn't go into her ward and allow Jack to go in himself. However, she asked him to tell me that she needed to see me. At that point she demanded that I supply her with a key to the house, told me that she intended to pick-up Jack one day that week and asked me for 'an interim settlement'. She told me that she had 'consulted' on these matters. Jack later told me that she said she was going into school with her father to collect him and take him with her one day that week.

At that time, she couldn't walk without the

aid of a frame. However, she continued to make progress and I believed she could soon be back on her feet. I took her threat seriously and informed the school. They agreed that Jack be collected only by my parents or myself. Jack was distressed by

what she'd said and was determined to stay with me. There was no doubt that, if she managed to get access to him, she would stop him returning to me. My immediate concern was to protect Jack and secure his future with me, if only by getting a temporary residency order. My case had to be that she was an unfit mother and I was prepared to produce all the evidence I had to support this. In short, I needed to protect Jack and myself against her.

Judith was temporarily released from hospital on 10th December, having been there for around two months. The following day she called me to insist that she and her parents collect Jack from school the next day (Friday) and take him to their house for tea. I had no legal right to withhold him or obstruct contact and so agreed - on condition that I be able to collect him afterwards. Whilst this was risky, it was also a confidence building move. If I did get him back, the principle would be set for future access. If he didn't come back, then I at least knew where I stood. In the end, all went well. I got Jack back and was then content that the future pattern would be with Jack staying with me during the week. Weekends would be her time with him.

Unfortunately, two days before Christmas, things erupted again. Judith had been demanding access to the house to get some

of her documents and clothing. I didn't want her near the place and so, that evening, I bagged her clothes and the papers, took them and dumped them outside the door of her parents' home for her. She reacted extremely badly to this and called me to demand that I return them to the house. She also insisted that I took Jack to her. I refused because she was incapable of caring for him. I lost my temper and accused her of being a lousy mother. Dick then intervened to demand that I return Jack. He was swearing, aggressive and threatened to beat me up. I cut the conversation off. I knew now that, if they gained access to Jack, I wouldn't see him again. I began to consider taking out an emergency residency order and arrange for supervised access for her and her family.

Christmas came. I put on the best show I could for Jack and he lacked for nothing. However, I had contracted pneumonia and the symptoms were showing by Christmas Eve while we were at a Carol Service. I struggled through Christmas Day but became very ill. I had no choice than to let

Jack go to his grandparents. I was in no condition to care for him and was bedridden for another two weeks. During that time, he stayed with them and the process of eliminating me from his life began again.

LOSING JACK – PART TWO

Since leaving hospital, Judith had been in contact with the Gateshead local authority and managed to get them to pay for a privately rented flat near Jack's school, in early February. She was placed on the top rate of disability benefit, didn't pay rent or council tax and received child tax credit and child benefit. Money shouldn't have been a problem to her. However, the heavy drinking resumed, as did the waste. Jack had come back to me during the week and saw Judith on a Saturday and Sunday. He told me that she was in the habit of taking him by taxi to a MacDonalds Drive Thru' - rather than make him anything to eat because she said she couldn't work-out how to use the oven! She took a taxi the few hundred yards to the local supermarket - where she would buy miniature bottles of vodka. Usually, she would take Jack and a few friends along and treat them to sweets to disguise the real nature of her 'mission'. On one occasion, I happened to be in the shop at the same time. She came up to me while my back was turned. I knew it was her, however, from the foul stench of stale vodka which drifted up the aisle before her.

The new access arrangements seemed to be working at that stage and I was doing my best to treat her kindly. I even bought her a crockery set as a housewarming gift. On Saturday 7th February however, there was an incident which placed Jack in real danger.

He told me a few days later that she'd been drunk and fell over in the flat. She was lying unconscious on the floor. Jack had a friend sleeping over, and I thought this was concerning on it's own, because she'd only one bedroom (and one bed) in operation. He said that the two of them couldn't wake her or lift her, so he called Dick and Janet. Judith woke and reacted extremely angrily. She was verbally aggressive to him and both the boys were very frightened. The two of them fled the apartment at around 8pm through a bedroom window. They stayed outside, in deep snow in another part of the street for around an hour, waiting for Dick to arrive. Dick stayed with them at the flat overnight but nothing hand changed and I was still concerned for Jack's welfare and safety. I tried to get more information out of Jack. He described the amount of wine that was lying around the flat, in cups but said he knew it was wine by the smell. I asked him why he hadn't called me, to be told that he was afraid of what his mam would have done because she had threatened him that he mustn't tell me ANYTHING.

I tried to stop him returning to the flat. However, this caused so much upset and her reaction caused great stress and anxiety to him, especially when she threatened to collect him from school and stop me seeing him again. I tried to playthings calmly and friendly but, unfortunately, it's impossible to reason with unreasonable people. The attempt to keep things on an even keel for Jack's sale was all one way. I said I'd allow him to return to her on condition that she remained sober and didn't interrogate him. She was furious.

The following week, I was stopped from seeing Jack and denied access. After that, any attempt I made to have him with me him was met with hostility and they often arranged to send him somewhere else. He was left very distressed and his welfare and education began to suffer. Because of the trauma he was experiencing, I didn't want to press the matter for fear of damaging him further. The divorce proceedings were underway again after the false start the previous year, thanks to Judith's hospitalisation. I thought it best to leave everything to the court.

After much arguing and pressure, I eventually managed to get an agreement to see Jack on a Saturday and Sunday, although this turned out to be a hit-and-miss affair. I gradually became aware that Judith and her parents were now taking him back to their house in Northumberland each night, after school. Judith was incapable of looking after him on her own and, each day they travelled the 15 miles there and 15 miles back. At first, they returned him on the few Saturday mornings I was allowed to see him. The three of them played a ruthless mind-bending game with Jack. I was in regular contact with the school and the teachers assured me that he was part of a close circle of good friends. However, Jack began to tell me that he hated them. Janet and Judith actively turned him against his friends, bad mouthing them and continually criticising them. When he was taken to his grandparents' home, he was encouraged to develop a new circle of friends there. Eventually, he told me that he had no friends at home because they all hated him. The three of them continued to slag me off in front of Jack. They interrogated him constantly whenever he returned after visiting me, they told him everything about the marriage breakdown and Judith even forced him to sit and read the divorce papers. At his young age, this was ridiculous and cruel. He told me that he had 'pretended' to read them but didn't really understand anything. Eventually, when he visited, he would ask questions which he'd obviously been told to ask by his mother and grandparents, about things that no child would ever think of. He questioned why I kept his mother short of money, whether I had been seeing someone else, how the business was doing ......

One Saturday, I went to the flat to collect him and he came out to the van to meet me. Judith had previously asked me for some of her papers from the house but hadn't given me enough notice to bring them that morning. Jack asked for the papers and I told him that I hadn't had time to look for them. I would bring them when we came back, the following day. He went back into the house to tell her what I'd said. He returned, *"Dad - I'm not allowed to go with you if you haven't brought the papers!"*. Again, I told him I'd be bringing them the following day. He returned to Judith, only to be sent out with the same response. He was getting very upset and I wasn't getting through to her because she was ruthlessly using him yet again. I told him I was sorry and that it might might be best if we let this weekend go. I watched as he forlornly shuffled back into the house.

I drove off, contact with Jack having been stopped again, although this 'reason' was a first. Moments later, Judith called me, ranting that I'd upset Jack. She said he was crying and sitting on the kerb outside. *Why had I left him in the middle of the road? I was 'pathetic' and 'no kind of father'. Why was I using him like that?*

On 8th March, Jack let it slip that they planned to move him permanently to Northumberland and to put him in a new school. The reason was that he was being 'bullied' again. In fact, this was manipulation as Janet had already alienated him from his friends and I was furious. I hadn't been consulted and was totally opposed to moving him out of the excellent Whickham Parochial School. I met with Jack's headmaster and, as usual, received his full support and cooperation.

I called Judith and she admitted that it was their plan because she couldn't cope on her own. I let her know how opposed I was, saying that it would be disastrous to upset him again and interrupt his education. He needed to be with his friends and he needed stability. In addition, he would be moved miles away from me, but she wouldn't listen.

I was very worried about Jack being thrown back into the type of atmosphere in which he'd suffered for so many years. I met my solicitor and had a letter sent to Judith's side. We pointed-out that I'd been as cooperative as possible and had even tolerated the reversal in access arrangements. My proposal was that Jack should remain with Judith, at her flat near the school, during the week. If that wasn't possible. I needed to know why (meaning, if she was incapable, then he should be with me). We made it clear that we had no objection to Jack spending time at his grandparents' but that we expected him to spend the majority of his time, during term time, at the flat and close to his school where he was making good progress. The solicitor also raised the issue of my loss of regular contact and went on to try to remedy this by stating that I'd collect him from the flat each Friday evening and return him each Sunday evening. We asked that Jack would be contactable on his mobile, a courtesy which she'd also have. There would always be a need for flexibility, especially around holiday time and it had to be agreed that neither of us would bad-mouth each other or our families, in front of Jack. I asked for a promise that she wouldn't drink excessively while Jack was in her care. We said that all the proposals were in Jack's best interests.

We received a letter from Judith's solicitor a week later, stating that she agreed to the arrangements 'in principle'. I was then able to pick up Jack the following Saturday (not Friday as agreed). On the Sunday though, he was very reluctant to return to Judith and told my parents that she *'was always shouting at him'*. He told me that he wanted to go back to the previous access arrangements, but I'd already made an agreement and tried to explain to him why that wasn't possible. Judith called and made a fuss because we were running 30 minutes late (a bit rich because she hadn't given me access until Saturday). She wanted me to give Jack money for *'his food and drink'!* At that time, the shops were closed, apart from off licenses. I suspected she needed money for alcohol and, instead, sent him back with some food and juice. This went up like a lead balloon and she became very agitated.

The following day, I called the school to check if Jack had turned up. He hadn't. I called him and was interrupted by Judith. She said that he had been upset that morning and was *'hurt and sore all over'* having *'tripped over a kerb'* the previous evening after I dropped him off. I had grave doubts about what had really happened but wasn't able to see him because Judith and her parents were again taking him away that evening. She then told me that she wanted Jack to be with her the following weekend of Mother's Day. I refused as weekends were my time with him. Besides, I wanted to get to the bottom of what had happened today. She reacted furiously and threatened to keep him away from me during holiday weekdays. She also tried to justify this with some ridiculous allegation about me stopping Jack from waving to one of his friends when we passed them in the van, a couple of weeks previously.

A few days later, my solicitor received a letter from Judith's side. She was demanding that Jack spend that weekend with her. I desperately wanted the access arrangements to work and said that I'd be prepared to reconsider PROVIDED that she agreed FULLY to the arrangements we'd made in future. On her behalf, her solicitor agreed, but, within 4 days, all telephone contact with Jack had been stopped again. All of the other points in the 'agreement' were also broken.

On 5th May, I told my solicitor that the arrangements had broken down. I'd agreed to Jack living with his mother, on the grounds that she'd fully recovered from her life threatening brush with alcohol and that she'd stopped drinking. I'd assumed she was capable of looking after him in her own home but didn't agree to him effectively living with his grandparents and regarded them as unsuitable 'guardians'. They were an evil influence and had interfered too much in his life. Furthermore, Judith's relationship with her mother had been known to be volatile and violent, in front of

Jack. His grandparents had a record of keeping Jack from me and attempting to influence and manipulate him against me. They were his grandparents and didn't have superior rights over me, his father.

I was totally opposed to Jack being moved to a school in Northumberland. That would be an unfamiliar environment, away from his friends and classmates. He would miss the opportunity to go to one of two excellent secondary schools in Whickham and he would be further isolated from me. The move would be purely for the convenience of his mother and grandparents. By constantly taking him to Sandhill, they were isolating him from his circle of friends in Whickham and at school. He was being forced to restrict his circle to children in Sandhill. At best, this would damage his existing friendships and, at worst, was a deliberate attempt to get him to agree to moving away.

Judith had to be reminded that she'd agreed that Jack should live mainly in Whickham for the sake of his schooling and that his routine wasn't disrupted by unnecessary travelling. He had to be allowed to mix with children in his own environment. I had to have free telephone access to him at reasonable hours. She was aware of my objections to him being moved to a new school and that I'd be prepared to take any necessary steps to safeguard his education.

On 6th May, a letter was therefore sent to Judith's solicitors. On 11th May, they replied. They stated that, while Judith and Jack did spend time at Dick and Janet's, they still lived at the flat. They denied that the 2-hour travelling time each day was a problem for Jack. They rejected the 'allegation' that Jack wasn't being allowed to mix with his friends at home or that his phone was switched off, or that he was being prevented from speaking to me. They confirmed that they 'unequivocally' gave her assurance that she'd *'ceased to be alcohol dependent'*. They were *'irritated'* at my *'continued suggestion that she still drank to excess'*. They categorically stated that there were no immediate plans to move to Northumberland - or move Jack to a new school.

8 weeks later, he was gone. I wasn't to see or speak to him again for six months.

GONE

I continued to try to call and text Jack. I was desperate, lonely and these were the blackest of days. If he had died, I think the pain of losing him would have been less intense.

I began to receive a torrent of texts from Judith, making wild and outrageous allegations and comments about me, questioning what I was doing, my finances and what happened to Jack when he was with me. I found this highly upsetting and I knew that Jack was being told many lies about me and my family. My texts to him were being intercepted and even deleted before he got them. There were also texts pretending to be from him. One day, totally out of the blue, I received " *Whatever I have said about my Mam I was saying it because I was mad and it is not true*".

I sent a message back:

"*What are you talking about, son?*"

"*You know*" was the response.

"*I don't because you've never said anything to me* ", I replied, knowing full well who I was actually chatting with.

After 10pm that night, Jack called me and repeated that whatever he had said wasn't true. His voice was strained and his manner simply wasn't like him. I asked him again what he meant. He told me that he had seen a letter from Judith's lawyer which had said he had been *'saying things'* about her the month before. He said that this had come from my solicitor. This was clearly ridiculous and I assured him again that he'd never said anything to me and that I had no idea what that had been about. Then he said, *"I thought I hadn't!"*. I told him that, even if he had said anything, I wouldn't tell anyone. With that, the phone went dead. I tried to call back. That confirmed my suspicion, that someone had been sitting over him, controlling what he'd been saying.

For a short while, I discovered I could speak to Jack via Facebook. Then, I found that the conversations were getting a bit 'weird'. He would try to lure me into saying derogatory things about his mam or his grandparents, he'd ask details about the divorce and the sale of the house, or about the business. Part way through the conversations, *"IT'S JUDITH - NOT JACK!"* would suddenly appear. In the end, I didn't know who I was talking to. She was obviously pretending to be him and on the occasions it *was* Jack, it was obvious that many of the words were hers. Eventually, she made him delete me from his Facebook account and so, even this means of contact was then dead.

I couldn't bear to think of him suffering as some kind of pawn in a sick game of chess, so I decided not to pursue access in order to save him further distress and myself, continued torment.

I'd found out that the school Jack now attended had arranged a couple of meetings to discuss his 'situation' with the staff. Academically he continued to do well but his attendances had slumped. The second meeting had been called to discuss the impact of his mother's drinking habits. Later, I discovered that he'd also been admitted to hospital suffering from a serious intestinal infection which kept him in isolation for two months, but no-one had informed me. I continued to send messages, letters and gifts but was never sure whether he got them. I even asked the school to pass-on a note I wrote for him but, after taking legal advice, they declined to do that.

I was to see Jack only twice more between June and December - once at October half term when we went to Center Parcs for a weekend and again in late November. On the last occasion I noticed great changes in him and not just physically. It was extremely difficult to make a connection with him and this was no doubt because he knew full well that he'd be grilled when he returned to his mother and grandparents. He also asked lots of pointed questions about the sale of the house and about the business. I sensed that the closeness we'd shared over the years despite all our problems, had weakened and he was distant now. I desperately wanted to be a good father but I also knew that, if he stood a chance of developing into a well-rounded adult, he had to be shown that there was more to life than 'things' and being 'bought off'. He had to be shown the value of life and its experiences. I then did something which I passionately believed to be right, but which rebounded badly.

Christmas was 5 days away. Jack kept asking me to take him to Toys R Us and buy him something – he wasn't sure what he wanted, he just WANTED something. He had been spoiled like that for years by his mother and grandparents. I'm certain that he was even told to do this by Judith before he met up with me. I refused but said that we could go into the shop and he could point-out the things that he would like for Christmas. That was probably naive of me. When we got there, he spotted a Ben 10 toy for £7.99 and pestered the life out of me to buy it. I refused firmly, telling him that Christmas was in a few days and that was the time for presents. When we got outside, he threw a hissy-fit. This was the first time Jack had ever acted like this when he was with me. I took him home and made tea but he continued to sulk and the atmosphere was very difficult. He asked if he could call his mam. I heard him complaining to her that I hadn't bought him the toy and I heard her telling him how 'terrible' that was. "Never mind", "Granddad would buy it for him when he got back"!

Because of the strained atmosphere, I told him that I knew he was upset but tried to reason with him. Still, he sulked so I asked if he wanted to go back to his mam - and he said he did. Reluctantly and with a very heavy heart, I drove him back. I told him that, whatever was said about me, he had to remember that I loved him. He was the only person who mattered to me. My heart was heavy on the way home and I later learned that his granddad had indeed bought the toy the following day.

I tried to make-up for this episode at Christmas. I wasn't to see him on Christmas Day, but was allowed to pick him up on Boxing Day provided I returned him in the afternoon. She'd arranged for his friends to call for him at 4pm, so he had to be back for then. He told me that Dick and Janet had bought him "a £400 TV". When they bought him anything, they always told him the price first. Even he said that this was 'a bit expensive' but they told him "nothing's too expensive for you gorgeous!". They were always trying to 'outbid' me and my family, not that we took part in this sick contest.

I bought him as much as I could, bearing-in mind that business was very poor and I hadn't been able to draw a wage for 6 months. I asked Jack why he needed to go back the same day. He told me that it was because his Mam would *'go over the top'* and he was the only one who could *'calm her down'*. He said that his *'Grandma causes it'*.

At that point, he volunteered the truth about the episode of *'saying things'* about her which *'weren't true'*. She'd been grilling him aggressively, demanding to know if he had ever said anything critical about her to me. She got him to admit that he had and she'd made him cry.

I negotiated a stay overnight and we did have a great time. I'd bought him an archery set and a fishing kit. However, the best fun we had was playing games and building models. I returned him on 27th December. I'd done or said nothing which could cause him grief. I hadn't even mentioned his mam or his grandparents. I hoped that contact could resume in the New Year.

On New Years Eve, he called and told me that he, his mother and a 'friend' were staying in the Copthorne Hotel in Newcastle. I was gob-smacked that Judith could afford it given that she had hounded me because of her lack of money. Nevertheless, I said nothing and simply wished him a great time. He wished me a Happy New Year and ended the call.

On the morning of New Years Day, Jack called again. He said that his mother wanted to talk to me. She took the phone and said we had to talk about arrangements for Jack. I asked her what she meant and she then said something which tore my guts out.

"He doesn't want to see you anymore!"

I was stunned and could hardly speak.

"You're wicked - evil ....." I started, but she put the phone down. I couldn't leave it there .... I had to speak to him! I called back but the phone was now switched-off. For three hours I tried to call him, dialling virtually every minute. Eventually, Judith answered and I demanded to speak to Jack. She told me that he wasn't there because he was downstairs in the hotel. I asked her to make sure he called me back. He didn't - so I called again and I eventually got to speak to him.

"Is it true son - what your Mam said? You don't want to see me anymore?"

(voices in the background - long pause).

"Well - maybe sometimes" he replied very sheepishly.

My world had fallen in. I was distraught.

"I love you son"

"Bye dad"

With that, the phone went dead.

Those were the last words my son said to me. I wasn't to see him again for another 5 years.

MY FINAL LETTER TO JACK

I sat in the house for days. I was too numb to weep but tears continually ran down my face. Life was simply not worth it anymore.

Over the next two weeks, despite having a healthy order book at work thanks to recent insurance orders, I had to call-in the Liquidator because of non-payment by customers and because of the continued burden of Judith's debt to the company. Of course, this impacted on me personally because I was a director of the company. I had guaranteed the overdraft to the bank. In addition, I had been left with personal debts of over £90,000 as a result of the rampant spending during the marriage. I was forced to enter into a voluntary arrangement with my creditors and lost my house. Within two weeks, I had lost my home, my business and my son. To add insult to injury, Judith was seeking to get a financial settlement from me.

In May 2010, I moved into a rented cottage and started to draw my private pension in order to live.

I was to see Jack once more. Judith had moved into a house on her own with Jack. She contacted me to ask if I'd like to see him and of course I did! We made arrangements for that Saturday and she gave me her new address. When I arrived, she opened the door in tears. Jack had let it slip to Dick and Janet that I was coming and they beat me to it by half an hour, bundling him into a car and taking him away!

No-one would fill the gaping hole in my life which was left by him. I would always love him and be there for him if and when he needed me. All I can do now was make sure that I was prepared for that time. His bedroom at my cottage was there, with his own bed and bedding, waiting for him, along with the first present I ever got him - the teddy bear I bought the day he was born!

Two years later, I decided to write.

"Hi, son,

I want you to know that I've always loved you and always will

Things haven't turned out very well and not what I'd hoped and planned for you. I wanted bring you up surrounded by love and safety. I planned to share so much with you and prepare you for the journey that lies ahead. Now, I don't even know what size shoe you wear, what music you like, what food you eat.... or even if you ever think of me or even care! I've missed so much of you growing up and I can't get that back!

I can't explain or excuse what happened. I didn't want you to grow up being afraid and miserable. I was weak and let awful things happen but I thought I was protecting you as best I could. I was wrong. By working too long and not being there enough, you saw and heard things that no young lad ever should. I can only say that I tried. I tried to be the best dad I could but ended up being part of your pain and suffering. I fought-on, believing that I was protecting you but ended up hurting you. You shamed me when you told me that you didn't have a nice life and I knew then that the constant rows and other nasty stuff had to end. So, I left, telling you that I loved you and would always be there for you. However, I wasn't there. I tried so very hard to be at your side but, in the end, it wasn't to be. I let you down and I'm sorry.

I wasn't there to give you the support that every decent dad wants to give his son. All good parents want better for their children than they had themselves. If I can do nothing more, then here are some words of advice:

Know and understand that I love you. Yes, I got it terribly wrong - and none of it was your fault. You are the centre of my universe and, to me, the most important person who has ever lived.

Believe in yourself. You are as important as anyone else and can achieve anything you set out to. Remember also that other people are important too and, by respecting others, you'll have THEIR respect

..........BUT

Don't let anyone put you down or control you. These people are filled by their own problems and only make others feel miserable so they can they feel better about themselves. STAY CLEAR!

Don't be afraid of what life throws at you. See every problem as a chance to rise to the top. Man-made problems have man-made answers and every problem has a solution. With determination, a plan and bravery, there is no obstacle to stand in your way.

...... HOWEVER

There's no shame in being wrong or making a mistake. Trouble only follows when you cover-up your wrongs or don't learn from your mistakes. Don't be afraid to ask for help, you're not expected to have all the answers!

Trust your instincts and be honest to yourself. If your guts tell you that something or someone is wrong, then they WILL be wrong. If in doubt, don't do it! If things go wrong after you've started down a path and continue to get worse despite your best efforts, stop what you're doing and start again. Don't waste your life trying to 'patch' things together and don't complicate your life and the lives of others by trying to 'cover up' or lie. It's not worth it and will usually come back to haunt you.

Live your life for yourself - you owe nobody anything.

When you choose someone to spend your life with,

understand that you've been drawn to them for the person they are. Don't try to change them - or you'll destroy the very person you loved in the first place! If they love you, they must treat you in the same way. Only with that kind of relationship, can you start to live for each other, in love and trust.

If and when you have children, ignore all of the above! Your life is now their life. There's no take - only GIVE. Allow them to grow-up surrounded by love, security, and magic. Above all, remember that they are small people, with their own personalities and wishes. They come to us on loan — we don't own them! It's their job to be children and your job is to shield them from anything that could destroy that. You choose to bring them into the world and they're then your joy and your responsibility for the rest of your life,

Let go of the past and live for the future. Don't waste time and energy in being angry but remember where you've come from and where you've been. By knowing that, you'll know better which way to go next!

My life is full of shame and regret. Shame at the things I've done and regret over the things I haven't. But you are my greatest and most proud achievement. You are all I will leave behind - and EVERYTHING I will leave behind

Now - do the old bugger a favour and make a better job of it than me!

With all my love. DAD XX"

I put the letter in my desk drawer, where it remained. Even if he got it, it would just be another source of unhappiness.

A SOCIAL DISSERVICE

It was just after he'd returned to me when Judith was in hospital but before I got pneumonia. Jack found another letter in the house which he thought I should read. It was from Safer Families in Gateshead, which dealt with domestic violence and worked alongside the police and social services. It was addressed to Judith and dated just after the evening I'd kept Jack away when I'd found her slumped, drunk in the study chair. Referring to a *'a recent incident'*, they said that the police had referred her to the group. One sentence really made me see red:

"Should you become frightened again at any time in the future, please do not hesitate to dial 999, your details can then be passed to our Crime Intervention Services with your consent!

I was livid at the implication that I'd attacked her. So, I wrote to them and demanded to know what threat they thought I posed to Judith. I pointed out that they hadn't contacted ME when she attacked me on the Day of Winkles and was arrested! It was outrageous and once again, biased and prejudicial. Twenty days later, there'd been no reply, so I decided to call them instead. There was a great deal of confusion and they were baffled when I asked who would advise **me,** because *I* was the victim, not Judith! They agreed to appoint a care worker to meet with me.

I met with the care worker on two occasions and spoke to her on the telephone several times. I painstakingly detailed the history of our situation and my concerns. She promised to liaise with social services, describing my letters as *'well considered'* and *'purposeful'*. Unfortunately, the social services case officer was still Susan Taylor and she wasn't prepared to meet with her. They had a brief telephone conversation, but the care worker wouldn't tell me much about that. When I persisted, I discovered that there was a clear suspicion that I'd been violent towards Judith. Eventually, I got a reply from Safer Families three weeks later. It was full of nothing and made no attempt to answer my questions. They said that, when police officers attend a domestic violence incident, they ask the victim if they would like to be referred to the service. They informed me that they offered advice to both victims **and perpetrators**. The letter went on to 'confirm' that I had referred myself to the service within the past month that they'd appointed a case worker to me! They went on to apologise if their service hadn't met my expectations. At the least, one hand clearly didn't know what the other was doing but it smacked of a cover up and the implication was still that Judith had been the 'victim'. They and social services were wedded to their belief that, as the man, *I* was the guilty party.

After I'd finally left the family home, social services kept an active interest for a few weeks. I heard that they'd held a series of interviews with Judith, Jack and her parents. Each visit had come with plenty of warning to allow them time to 'prepare' and show a united front. They drilled and rehearsed Jack on what to say, to perfection. The department made no attempt to speak to me and so I wrote to them, thanking them for the interest they were taking in Jack but asking to be informed of what was going on, because of my concern for him.

A couple of weeks later, Susan Taylor called me to tell me that they were closing the case for a second time. She told me that she'd visited Jack the previous day and found no cause for concern, although he'd voiced some concern about his mother's drinking! She'd received my letter but told me that the case was being closed even after considering all the matters I'd raised. If I had concerns for Jack's welfare and safety, it was my responsibility to remove him from Judith's care and take any legal steps which may be necessary.

Ms. Taylor went on to claim that she hadn't

been contacted by anyone else about Jack's welfare, apart from one incident referred to by the police. This was the Day of Winkles attack which social services had now downgraded to a *'verbal altercation with a slight punch to the face'*. She told me that she'd be advising Jack's school of her decision, that day.

I told her I was astounded that a physical assault could be described as a minor argument, especially when Judith had been arrested for it! I knew that the police, Jack's school and our doctors had all registered their concerns long before this too. I asked why she'd given them long notice of the meetings and why she'd involved Dick and Janet when no other family members (including myself) had been interviewed or consulted. While I didn't agree with her decision and understood that she'd come to it in accordance with her professional judgement, I reminded her that this was also her professional <u>responsibility</u>. For so long as his mother was under the influence of alcohol, Jack would be at risk. When I reminded her that even the case worker from Safer Families in Gateshead had expressed the view that Jack was in a high-risk situation, she became very irritated. I asked that, if I'd been the mother rather than the father, would the case have been closed so readily? With that, Susan Taylor slammed the phone down on me.

I heard from Ms. Taylor again a few weeks later. She called me to ask if I could tell her more about Judith's admittance to North Tyneside General. The hospital reported that she'd been taken in by ambulance and they had concerns for Jack. Of course, I knew nothing about it and Susan Taylor wouldn't give me any details. I pointed out the hypocrisy of her call because she'd previously decided that the case was closed and dismissed my concerns! This time, she said she'd keep me informed. She didn't contact me again.

I discussed what had happened with my cousin who was a senior social worker in Northumberland. She was horrified at Susan Taylor's attitude. A short time later, I also discussed the matter in confidence, with a client who happened to be the Director of Children's Services in another county. She was also appalled and told me that she would have instantly sacked any member of her staff if they'd reacted in the way That Ms. Taylor had. Both urged me to appeal to the Director of Social Services.

On 10th June, I wrote to the Director and enclosed copies of all the relevant correspondence. I gave the reasons why Jack was at risk and listed all the agencies which had been involved and which had urged me to involve her department. I told her of the meetings I'd had with Susan Taylor and how I'd been met with hostility and prejudice. I detailed the history of what had happened and how I'd been excluded from meetings and updates. Furthermore, my own concerns had been brushed aside. I went on to describe how the case had been handled and ended by pleading to have it re-opened.

On 25th June, a letter arrived, informing me that the case was to be re-opened under a different social worker. It said that this was no reflection on Susan Taylor but thought that it was an opportunity for a new person to establish a 'working relationship' with me while they started a further assessment of Jack's situation.

Jane Fowler, the new social worker, made no attempt to get in touch with me. So, I wrote to her on 11th August to tell her that I hadn't seen Jack for 11 weeks and was worried about him. I offered to be available at any time to meet with her. She didn't reply.

On 10th September, I eventually received a letter from Ms. Fowler who claimed that she'd tried to telephone me without success! Her message was that the case was going to be closed again, for the third time!

She said that, over the past month *'or so, things had settled down'* with regards to Judith's drinking. She was satisfied that Judith had *'addressed the problem appropriately'*. Jack's needs had been met *'in the maternal home'* and she had no outstanding concerns.

Two weeks later, Ms. Fowler wrote to me again. Her department had just been contacted by one of Judith's friends expressing concern about Jack and her. She'd said that the home conditions were very poor and that Judith was drinking heavily. There was little food in the house for Jack or her and that there was little money for basic 'amenities'. Ms. Fowler then said she had written to Judith to *'offer advice'* and invited me to take action as I *'saw appropriate'* and invited me to call her to discuss the matter.

I was furious and really didn't want to speak to that bunch of prejudiced, blind-sided incompetents again, but forced myself for Jack's sake. I corrected her 'understanding' of the money situation and pointed out that she'd just raised **_exactly_** the concerns which had forced me contact the department in the first place! However, despite my best efforts, the case had been opened and closed on three occasions. I told her that they were close minded and prejudiced.

Months later, when I was sifting through the

pile of correspondence after I'd moved back home, I found the letter that Ms. Fowler had sent to Judith. She had made it clear to her that, if she continued to drink, she would have to re-open the case. Ironically, by the time her letter had been sent, Judith was already in hospital with acute liver failure. Ms. Fowler wasn't aware of this because she hadn't done even the smallest thing she HAD promised. She hadn't monitored the situation or maintained contact with Jack's school and so, on 10th October, I called her to give her both barrels. She was shocked at Judith's hospitalisation. I went on to tell her that Jack had been taken by his grandparents and that he was under their 'inappropriate' influence. This also had implications for his schooling because of the distances involved. He hadn't been to school the previous week and his teachers were aware of the situation. Had she done her job, she would have been fully aware of the position. I pointed out that _I_ should be caring for Jack, not his grandparents. Social services had previously insisted that I gave Judith access to Jack, so why hadn't they involved themselves in securing **_my_** access to him now? She told me that my access wasn't an issue for Social Services! I accused the department of a lack of communication, prejudice and incompetence. Ms. Fowler could say little to me, but I could detect that she was acutely embarrassed. I therefore decided to put yet another complaint in writing.

Two MONTHS later, I received a reply which simply said:

"We understand that you recently contacted Referral and Assessment Team regarding your son, Jack. Based on information you provided, we recommend that you contact your solicitor with these concerns. We are satisfied that as the parent with parental responsibility, it is in Jack's best interests to remain in your care"(?)

With that, Gateshead Social Services washed their hands of my son and walked away. However - I wasn't finished with THEM yet!

I studied the notes in Judith's handwriting which had been designed as 'coaching aids' for Jack. He was well drilled in what he had to say. One said:

"My Mam had one ambulance because she felt totally sic and dissy" (For a boy who apparently couldn't spell 'sick' or 'dizzy', his handling of 'ambulance' and 'totally', was pretty impressive!

I then found two pages of preparation notes, written by Janet but as if they had been prepared by Judith. I knew their different handwriting styles but, in any case, Janet slipped up on the second page by referring to 'Judith' in the third person.

They claimed that

- I'd broken Judith's arm
- physically and mentally abused her
- hid food in case Jack ate it and generally kept them short of food
- played mind games
- was a liar
- had disabled the gas fire and lights
- hid money at my parents' house
- I'd sent divorce papers to Judith
- 'Got rid' of her friends (presumably by chasing them away because they hadn't yet included murder on the list!)
- I wasn't very well liked and had no friends
- I came in from work and ignored Judith and Jack
- I wasn't 'very nice' to the cats
- I thought it was 'disgusting' that Dick and Janet had bought a phone for Jack
- my parents 'never came to see Jack'
- I fell off a ladder at work and told everyone that Judith had caused it
- I'd been drugging Jack
- I always quizzed Jack when he was with me

- Jack was afraid I wouldn't return him to his mother after he'd been with me
- It was 'shocking' that I'd wanted to take Jack camping with another 51-year-old man (my friend Dave) and his niece and nephew (whose mother had recently died from cancer).

I was furious that they'd been given enough notice to construct such a dossier of lies and distortions in advance of the meetings. Added to this, the department made no attempt to speak with me or my family. This was the final straw!

As I waded further through the pile, what I found next shook me to the core.

I came across a thick foolscap folder containing a set of official confidential, internal only, documents compiled by the social services team. These were the case notes on our family. Attached to the front was a compliment slip from Jane Fowler. It said:

"Dear Judith - please find enclosed a copy of the Core Assessment for you to read through. I would like to meet you on Thursday 4th September at approximately 1030am - Should this not be convenient, please do not hesitate to contact me. Jane Fowler"

How was the file in Judith's possession? I now had proof of the collusion between Judith, her parents and the department.

The file contained a catalogue of errors, mistakes and lies. Again, there were claims that there'd been no reports of concern received from any party except me. Yet, on page 2 it stated that the police had reported that *'the mother was undoubtedly suffering from an alcohol problem'*. They also chose not to mention the formal reports from our GP's, North Tyneside General Hospital or the concerns reported by the school. On a scale of 1-10 (10 being the best), Susan Taylor had assessed the danger to Jack from Judith's drinking at 7 while Jane Fowler downgraded it to 5. Ms. Taylor had put her concern for Jack's general well-being at 8 but Ms. Fowler hadn't assessed it at all. It admitted that Jack had expressed concerns about *'the wine and mam falling asleep'* and also recorded that Jack had told his class during a "show and tell' session that he'd seen his mother drunk. This could only have come from the school! It recorded the North Tyneside hospital report of Judith being admitted to hospital with an enlarged liver linked to alcohol misuse. There had been *'claims and counter claims'* from myself and Judith about assault and emotional abuse and Jack was worried about finance following our separation. As a result, he didn't want to see me and said that I was *'quizzing him about everything'*. The school **had** reported concerns about Jack's attendance and lateness, staff had smelled alcohol on Judith's breath and they'd received third party information about her drinking! The report went on to say that Jack had said that things at home were *'absolutely perfect'* (Judith's favourite catchphrase) and spoke lovingly of his Mam and described her as *'funny and kind'*. His grandparents had provided games in the house such as Scrabble and Monopoly (I'd bought these years ago). The maternal grandparents were 'actively involved' (as if that was a good thing!). Judith's 'presentation' was *'fine'* and her drinking was *'under control at present'*, She'd sought professional help for Jack because of the *'situation'* In fact, (I found several letters from that agency asking Judith why she had missed the appointments for Jack).

The notes went on to detail a 'Plan' which was to close the case because it was felt that Jack had a support network in place already. Jane Fowler would 'talk' to Dick and Janet about *'vigilance around drinking'* (talk about putting King Herod in charge of Mothercare!). She would also inform the school of her decision and ask them to refer any future concerns or any deterioration. Ms. Fowler would also 'update' me about the case - which, of course, she didn't, other than tell me it was being closed!

Jack's 'support network' was mapped out in a diagram. On the maternal side of the family, they had included Dick and Janet, her brother and sister-in-law and even Judith's 2-year-old niece. According to them, my side of the family comprised only of a pair of elderly and infirm parents. In fact, Jack later told me that they'd taken him separately and asked him to draw all his family members in a room, on a piece of paper and place the ones he felt safe with and wanted to be with, closest to him. He'd drawn me, my mam and dad, sister and niece around him, before placing Judith, Dick and Janet in the furthest corners of the room. This was never reported or included.

Within the report, Ms. Fowler repeated that *'things have calmed down'* over the past *'couple of months'*. She claimed that Jack saw **both** sets of grandparents but described my parents as *'horrible'*!. He spoke *'positively'* about Dick and Janet and regularly stayed with them. He *'presented'* as *'loyal'* to his family - particularly the *'maternal side'*.

Judith had reported that there were a lot of *'difficulties'* after the separation, financially. This included the phone and TV *'being stopped'* and this was *'impacting'* on Jack and he felt it was unfair. Ms. Fowler had asked

Judith to address this by speaking to a solicitor and get some form of interim financial settlement from me to *'ensure Jack's needs were met'*. She did say that she had also *'encouraged'* Judith not to talk about these matters in front of Jack as this was mainly 'adult business'.

In one paragraph, Jane Fowler seemed determine to undermine my efforts to ensure Jack's safety by portraying my concerns as nothing more than petty criticism:

"Mr. Allan reported that, on one particular evening in May, neighbours complained to him because Judith had friends round and apparently the house was untidy"

I wondered if she was either very cunning or entirely stupid. I decided it was the latter.

By contenting herself that *'things had settled down'*, that there were *'routines in place for Jack'*, that *his physical care needs were met'* and that he was *'adequately fed, dressed and bathed'*, no action was required. Indeed, *'Jack spoke very lovingly about his mother'* and *'appears to have a very close relationship to her'*

It continued. When Susan Taylor had spoken to Jack about the *'verbal altercation'*, his only concern had been that his mother *'fell asleep one or two times a month'*. He loved his mother but *'got a little anxious'*. Susan had given her *'advice' and visited again after* she'd been informed that Judith had been in hospital suffering from *'alcohol withdrawal'* - but again, they'd had a chat!

Ms. Fowler now believed that Judith's *'drinking issues'* had *'really improved'* since then and what *'kept her going'* was being away from me and the arguments which were what *had 'turned her to drink' in the first place*! Now, she couldn't *'afford'* to drink *and may have a 'couple of glasses, 2-3 times a week'*. She'd even asked Jack why he'd said in school that he'd seen his mother drunk. He'd replied that he'd only done it because he was *'angry'* about *'the situation'*.

There were more lies and contradictions. Ms. Fowler noted with satisfaction that there was a trampoline and basketball ring in the garden which Jack was allowed to play-on, *'on a supervised basis'*. In fact, both items had been bought by Dick and Janet and dominated the garden. They were too big and the trampoline was very dangerous, being pushed up against a sharp and low garden wall (there was nowhere else for it). Jack and his friends were allowed to play on it at all hours and in all weather, usually when Judith was pissed and out of it.

She went on to say that Jack was set boundaries in terms of playing outside –

what he could and couldn't do. She didn't want to underestimate the *'severity'* of Judith's drinking problem, but that Jack described his Mam as being *'absolutely perfect'* - that phrase again! Judith reported that Jack didn't want to phone me and told Ms. Fowler that he didn't want to see me because he was *'angry about the financial situation'*. Judith and her parents had said that Jack was a *'popular boy at school'*. He had 'many relationships with various peers' and *'spoke about them'*. (These being the same friends who were bullies and 'nasty' and were why he needed to move away to Northumberland!).

She concluded by saying that Jack *'presents as quite an anxious boy'* and that *'he is likely to be quite impressionable in terms of what is taken on in what he may hear in conversations'.'* He appeared to be *"very impressionable in terms of his views of people and at present seems to be quite angry with his father around his parents' separation and contact with him"*.

The irony of all this, of course was that, even as the ink dried on the report, Judith had drunk herself to the point of oblivion and was lying in intensive care.

I put this all to the back of my mind for a while. However, in May, I wrote to the Director of Children's Services at Gateshead and asked for an explanation of how these documents ended up in Judith's possession. I was told that it was 'normal procedure' when a case was closed i.e. to send a copy of the notes to the main carer. Of course, at that point, the case hadn't been closed. They'd decided it WOULD be closed but needed more 'confirmation' from Judith and her parents to do that. They hadn't involved me and I believed that I too, should certainly have received a copy!

My last letter to Gateshead Social Services was on 19th May:

"I would like to raise with you, one last damning point. You informed me that my wife's drinking had 'settled down' and had been 'addressed appropriately'. Only 20 days later, you wrote to her, having been contacted by a 'friend'. You expressed concern that she was drinking again and indicated that you may need to become involved once more. At around the same time, my wife was admitted to hospital with liver failure brought on by alcohol misuse. She fell into a coma and was not expected to survive.

My son's maternal grandparents (who had denied me any contact with him for several months previously) then took him into their own care without my knowledge or consent. I did not find-out about these events until 3 weeks later. I contacted you and, despite your assurance that action would be taken if my wife's alcohol problem re-occurred, you did not act. My wife eventually recovered in January and the council provided private rented accommodation for her. Soon after, Jack and a friend had to escape through a window in his mother's flat on a winter's evening, once again because of her drunken behaviour. I informed you about this at the time but was told that you would have taken further action only if the police had been informed first.

My wife and Jack now live at her parents' home in Northumberland because she cannot cope on her own. Jack still attends Whickham Parochial School and this involves him waking early each day and travelling to school at 7 o'clock each morning. You will be relieved that Jack is beyond the jurisdiction of the authority now. I do not wish to involve you further in his welfare because I have no confidence in your impartiality or competence.

From the day I approached you for assistance. I was confronted by doubt and prejudice. I was asked whether I was simply 'having a bad day' and asked why I was complaining about 'the woman who had brought up my child for eight years'. This outrageous question implied that I had no role in Jack's upbringing. In that simple moment of clarity, your prejudice from the very start, was abundantly clear"

I had gone to them for help, having real concerns about Jack's safety and wellbeing, only to be met with hostility and suspicion. They were prejudiced and got it wrong because their minds were closed. They got the facts wrong and, as so-called 'professionals' had allowed themselves to be manipulated and duped. They conspired with the very people who were the cause of the problem. Their report proved that they had doubts but, by that time, they'd ploughed their own furrow. They needed the case to go away. Denial didn't make it right; they were negligent and institutionally prejudiced. They were flat wrong and, in the end, they failed a child and added to his suffering.

I received no reply and had no further contact with Gateshead social services.

EPILOGUE

Judith passed away on 14th June 2013, a day after her 45th birthday. I wasn't told about it, but my mother read the obituary in the local newspaper a week later. She called me to let me know and, of course I was deeply shocked but not entirely surprised. After a few minutes, my thoughts turned to Jack. How was he? Was he OK? What was happening?

I'd been paying maintenance to Judith, directly into her bank account. Thinking about his financial security, I called the Child Support Agency to let them know that Judith had died and that I needed to make arrangements for Jack. I wanted to know If I could pay directly into his own bank account. It was shocking to hear that they'd already been informed by Janet who had asked for my payments to be diverted into her own account. The really disturbing part was that she'd done this only the day after Judith had died! They'd told her that they couldn't do that without my permission, much to her annoyance.

I tried really hard to track Jack down. It had been years since we'd spoken but I eventually had a Facebook request accepted. We arranged to meet up in the village he was living in. Before I went up, I bought him a new smartphone because it was important that we kept in touch now. He wanted to meet in the car park of the local pub, which I found strange until the reason became obvious. My heart was pounding as I approached and looked for him. I couldn't see him, only a few older teenagers on bikes. Of course, I was looking for the boy I remembered and, when one of the tall lads with long hair approached my car, I was taken aback! I hardly recognised him now! I opened the car door and was tempted to hug him but I could see that he was uncomfortable and his eyes kept darting towards the pub windows. I asked him to get into the car, but he wouldn't. The conversation was awkward and strained as I asked him how he was and what had happened although he was reluctant to say much. We struggled on with the conversation awkwardly for around 20 minutes, but I could see that he really didn't want to go on. We did agree to meet up again, though and I left, reluctantly.

A week later, I picked him up from a bus stop in the same village. He was looking behind himself, awkwardly. After he got in the car, we went off to South Shields for the afternoon and this was a very different Jack. It was almost as if we had never been apart as we bonded again. He told me about how his mam had deteriorated quickly after they'd been to Center Parcs. He'd noticed how her eyes had turned yellow and pleaded with her to go to the doctors. She did that when they returned and was immediately hospitalised. She never came out. Jack was much more matter of fact about it and hadn't really grieved for her. The truth was, as he later told me, it had come as something of a relief — from the violence and arguments between her and her mother and because he didn't have the burden of caring and *'looking out for her'*.

He also told me that the reason he was nervous when we met up was that he'd been warned not to get into my car because I would 'abduct' him at that first meeting. Dick and Janet obviously knew about it but had other things on their mind. Therefore, they'd sent their friend Debra to accompany him. She was sitting in the pub watching us, ready to pounce. If she did pounce, I would be in trouble. Not only had she threatened to kill me before but a 'pounce' from her would leave me with many crushed organs and broken bones. Today's meeting had been in secret, he hadn't told anyone where he was going.

During the days to come, I had to figure out a way of stopping Dick and Janet blocking my access to Jack. Knowing the type of people they were, I hit on a plan. I wrote to them to send my sympathies and to try to bury the hatchet. The real point was to make them an offer. If they'd allow me weekly access to Jack, I'd pay the maintenance into Janet's account. All I needed was her bank details. The following Saturday, I met him again and he gave me a piece of paper with the account details written on it.

Jack and I continued to rebuild our relationship. As we did so, he told me of the horrendous situation between Judith and her parents ... the arguments, violence, police visits, neighbours getting involved out of fear for him, his continual illnesses and deteriorating academic performance, his 20% school attendances and the fights with fellow classmates as they ribbed him about his mother being a drunk.

Because he was setting out on his GCSE courses, we discussed and agreed that it would be best for him to stay on at his school and, therefore continue to live with his grandparents, but backed up by my presence in his life now. We worked very hard on his attendance and school work, to the point where he aced business studies and stood miles ahead of his classmates. When it came to his A levels, we tried to move him to an academy near me but he couldn't settle. So, he went back to his school in Northumberland and his grandparents. On his 17th birthday, I bought him a car and driving lessons, Together with the weekend driving with me, he passed first time and was able to come and go as he liked. His confidence and freedom were building.

Having passed his A levels, there was a sudden change in the family dynamic. His grandmother started to give him a really bad time and made his life a misery once more, telling him she hated him and to '*get out*'. The change in her attitude towards him was savage but we realised, of course, that this all tallied with the end of her payments for Child Benefit and Tax Credits. Jack no longer served 'a purpose'. And so it was that he came back to the 'family home' that year.

Although we were happy to be together again, life was tough because Jack was never 'quite right' in the sense of his health. We couldn't bottom out what was causing his breathing problems and exhaustion, along with a myriad of other symptoms. Things took a turn for the worse in early 2020 and, worryingly, coincided with the COVID era when it was impossible to get near a doctor to begin the right program of tests. Instead, we had to endure and suffer telephone consultation after telephone consultation for the next 3 years with diagnoses range from postnasal drip and 'health anxiety' to multiple sclerosis and liver failure. Only after COVID restrictions were lifted did we get in front of a doctor who knew what they were about and a sizeable and awkward hole in the heart was detected! He'd also had a dose of COVID early on and this, ironically, allowed the hole to be detected while it had gone unnoticed throughout his childhood. He subsequently had a closure operation and began to recover quickly. He may not be quite out of the woods yet, but we're a long way from those dark days. It's a sad indictment that his health problems were probably the result of fetal alcohol syndrome!

So, here's my message of hope to all the selfless, caring dads out there who have cruelly suffered the torture of being alienated from their children.

First, know that the sins of these wicked controllers will find them out! Such as the time Jack, while looking for something of his many months later, rummaged in the back of his grandparents' wardrobe to find scores of letters from me to him. Despite them telling him for years that I'd abandoned him, there were my weekly letters telling him how much I loved and missed him and keeping him up to date with what was going on with me and my family. Each letter had money stuffed into it so that he could buy what he wanted. By the time he found them, they had all been opened and the money taken!

Second, and most important of all, know that kids ain't daft!!! All the way through, Jack knew EXACTLY what was happening and, more than that, had analysed it, rationalised it and made up his own mind. He loved his mam but knew she was ill and couldn't fight back against her mother, who he now loathed with a passion! While Janet now lies in a secure hospital having succumbed to alcohol induced dementia, Dick wallows alone at home, the only subject of conversation he has when speaking to Jack, being Janet. Jack and I have now been living under the same roof as a family for the past 8 years. We have a home which no one can take from us again and have built a successful small family business together. Now, I can be happy in the knowledge that we have moved on and his future is finally secure and bright .... and that, as they say, is where we came in!

Printed in Dunstable, United Kingdom